BLACK AFRICA COOK BOOK

RECIPES BY
MONICA BAYLEY
ILLUSTRATIONS BY
ALAIN LE FOLL

BLACK AFRICA COOK BOOK
FIRST PAPERBACK EDITION
MAY, 1977
(New Material Added)
First Edition 1971

Library of Congress Catalogue Card Number: 77-78297

PUBLISHED AND COPYRIGHT © 1977 BY
DETERMINED PRODUCTIONS, INC.
BOX 2150, SAN FRANCISCO
CALIFORNIA 94126
WORLD RIGHTS RESERVED
PRINTED IN THE U.S.A.

Not American soul food, this is authentic tropical African cooking. Monica Bayley and fellow gourmets the Le Folls (Alain's drawings spice up the book) took a cook's tour across the middle of the continent, starting in Ethiopia and on through Kenya, Uganda, Tanzania, Ghana and Senegal. This book is the delicious result of their busy forks and pens. Ingredients have been Americanized and all recipes carefully tested so that all the flavors and tastes of black Africa cooking pots, ovens and kitchens are here to enjoy.

CONTENTS

CHILIES

SNACKS
13 Yam Fritters
14 Samosas
15 Kaklo
16 Akara
16 Peanut Butter
18 Lamb Snacks

SOUPS
19 Hot Peanut Soup
19 Cold Avocado Soup
20 Red Bean Soup
21 Cold Soup
22 Sambhar Soup

SALADS
24 Salade des Iles
25 Salade Africaine
25 Papaya Mold
26 Papaya Salad
26 Avocado Salad
26 Congo Avocado
27 Avocado Salad
28 Shellfish Salad
29 Mayonnaise

MEATS
32 Shoko
33 Couscous
35 Ghana Stew
36 Zighini
36 Chichinga
37 Mchuzi
38 Biriani
40 Groundnut Stew
41 Bondo Gumbo
41 Bania Bamia
42 Laham Maa Curry
43 Kale Nyama
44 Brinjalburgers
46 Forfar Bridies

POULTRY
- 47 Yassa au Poulet
- 48 Groundnut Stew
- 49 Groundnut Stew
- 50 Ethiopian Hot Wat
- 51 Coconut Chicken
- 52 African Gumbo
- 53 Jolof Rice
- 54 Groundnut Chicken

SEAFOOD
- 56 Thiou au Poisson
- 57 Ntorewafroe
- 58 Seafood Stew
- 60 Fish Curry
- 61 Coconut Sauce Cod
- 62 Fish Cakes
- 63 Lemon Cold Fish

BREAD
- 66 Quick Bread
- 66 Likoma Easy Dough
- 67 Enjera
- 68 Corn Cakes
- 69 Corn Fritters
- 70 Banana Bread
- 71 Rice Bread
- 72 Peanut Muffins

MASHES
- 74 Fufu
- 75 Matoke
- 75 Futali
- 76 Irio
- 76 Touo
- 77 Ugali
- 77 Ugali
- 78 Water Bread

RICE
- 80 Savory Rice
- 81 Steamed Rice
- 81 Spicy Rice
- 82 Yellow Rice I
- 83 Yellow Rice II
- 83 Rice Cakes

VEGETABLES & SAUCES
- 85 Mais de Mombasa
- 86 Burundi Beans
- 86 Chad Squash
- 87 Dun Dun
- 88 Ndiwo
- 88 Mchicha
- 89 Bajias
- 90 Mchicha
- 91 Groundnut Sauce
- 91 Kobeywa
- 94 Palava
- 95 Palava
- 96 Curried Meat Sauce
- 97 Pilli Pilli
- 97 Pilli Pilli Mayonnaise

CHUTNEYS & RELISHES
- 99 Red Chutney
- 99 Green Chutney
- 100 Papaya Chutney
- 101 Tamboule
- 102 Hot Carrot Relish
- 102 Cucumber Sambal

DESSERTS
104 Tapioca
105 Top Bananas
105 Banana Boats
106 Mango Mousse
106 Coconut Pudding
107 Banana Crêpes
108 Macaroons
110 Puff Puffs
111 Gali Akpono
112 Chin Chin
114 Apricot Cream
114 Fruit Whip
115 Groundnut Pastry
116 Ghana Pumpkin Pie
117 Sweet Potato Pie
118 Coconut Cake

BEVERAGES
120 Coconut Milk
121 White Elephant
121 Ethiopian Punch
122 Pineapple Cooler
123 Pineapple Punch
124 Punch Ouaga
124 Orombo
124 Lemon Squash
125 Frosted Cocoa
125 Hot Cocoa

ILLUSTRATIONS

- 11 Rhino, Kenya Early in the Morning
- 17 Cooking Inside
- 23 Fishermen on the Beach Near Zanzibar
- 30 Cattle
- 39 Fruit and Vegetable Market, Dakar
- 45 Chicken and Egg Market
- 55 Fish on Beach
- 59 Fisherman in Indian Ocean Near Tanzania
- 64 Mammy Wagons Going to Market, Accra
- 73 Fufu, West Africa
- 79 Water Seller, Dar es Salaam
- 84 Spice Market
- 92 Cooking in the Compound
- 98 Masai Girls, East Africa
- 103 Turkana Tribe Warriors, North Kenya
- 109 Women from Dakar
- 113 Fruit Market Near Accra
- 119 Party
- 126 Women Walking on the Road to Masindi, Uganda

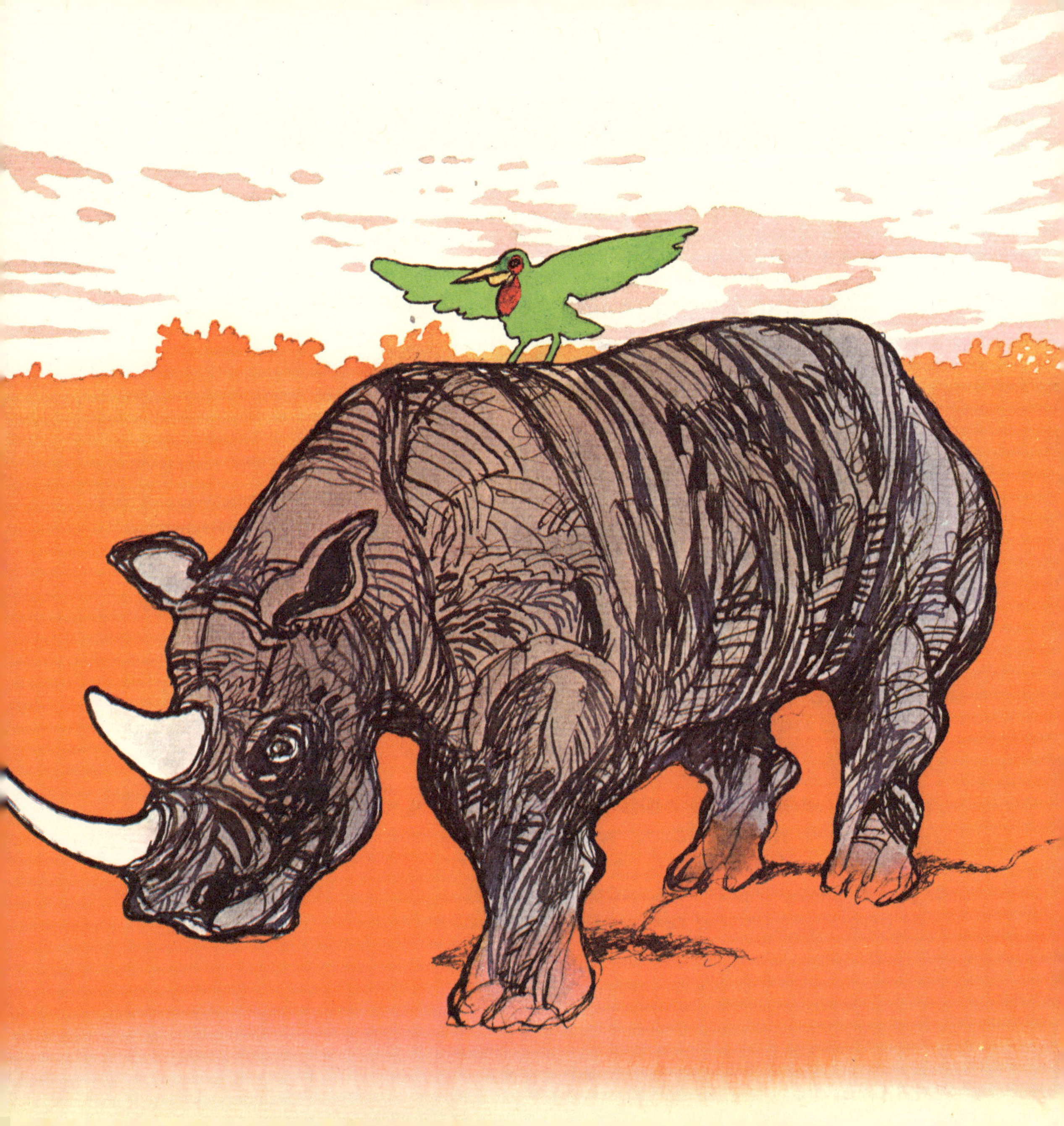

CHILIES

Many of the recipes in this book call for fresh green chili peppers or ground red peppers. Be careful in selecting and preparing them, for there are many kinds of chilies which vary in size, color and degree of hotness. The amounts in these recipes are calculated for medium-hot dishes. They may be increased or decreased to suit your taste. In Africa, most dishes are on the hot side. Try them this way, and if you think you want them hotter, increase the amount next time.

When recipes call for green chili peppers, use the mild 5 to 6-inch long California or Anaheim chilies, fresh or canned. When recipes call for *hot* green chili peppers, use medium-size 2 to 3-inch long Jalapeños, fresh or canned.

Wash under cold water, break off stems. Using a small sharp knife, scrape out seeds and rinse. Cut in half and lay skin side down on chopping board. Slice or chop very carefully and when you finish, wash your hands, the knife and the board in soapy water. Do not touch your face with your hands while preparing chili peppers.

Crushed, dried red chili peppers and ground red peppers are available in most stores where spices are sold. When recipes in this book call for dried red peppers use the small half-inch long dry red peppers and crush carefully in a mortar. Other recipes will specify ground red peppers or cayenne.

SNACKS

Africans who are too busy to stop working or too far away from home to prepare meals are fond of snacks. These food items are prepared ahead and then carried about and eaten cold when needed by field and plantation workers, school children and women who work away from their homes or villages. Snacks are also good served as appetizers for parties.

YAM FRITTERS

1½ pounds yams
1 egg, beaten
½ teaspoon salt
¼ teaspoon pepper
¼ teaspoon thyme
Pinch of cayenne pepper
½ green chili, seeded and minced
1 medium-size onion, chopped fine
1 medium-size tomato, chopped fine
½ cup bread crumbs
Peanut oil for frying

Boil yams with skins on until tender. Peel and mash smooth. Sauté chopped onion, tomato, and chili pepper in a few tablespoons oil until brown. Add seasonings and sautéed mixture to yams. Add beaten egg and bread crumbs and mix well. Form into small patties and sauté in peanut oil until brown on both sides.

SAMOSAS

(bits and pieces of cooked meat or fish in a thin crust made with curried flour)

FILLING

2 cups cooked meat, fish or chicken, chopped fine
½ cup onions, minced
½ teaspoon salt
⅓ teaspoon ground red chili pepper
½ small green chili pepper, minced (optional)

CRUST

1 cup flour
½ teaspoon curry powder
4 tablespoons margarine
4 tablespoons cold water

Sift flour and curry powder into bowl. Work margarine in with fork or fingertips until mixture resembles coarse meal. Add water and stir to form thick dough. Divide dough into 8 parts. Roll out each part into a very thin circle. Cut circles of dough into quarters. Mix filling ingredients together and put 1 teaspoonful of filling on each quarter circle of dough. Fold dough over filling in cone shape and crimp edges with fork or fingers to seal. Bake in 350° oven until golden brown. This makes 32 small samosas.

KAKLO

(banana snacks)

- 2 bananas
- 1 small onion, chopped
- 1 tomato, chopped
- ½ fresh chili pepper, seeded and minced
- ½ teaspoon salt
- 1 teaspoon grated ginger root
- 1 cup flour
- ⅛ cup water
- Peanut oil for frying

Peel bananas and mash. Add chopped onion, tomato and chili pepper and mash again. Add salt and ginger. Mix flour and water, then add mash and stir well. Heat oil until hot enough for deep-frying. Drop mixture half-teaspoonful at a time into oil and fry until golden brown. Balls should be crisp on the outside, but soft on the inside. Serve as hot or cold snacks, or hot with a main dish.

◀ AKARA ▶

(bean balls)

- 2 cups cooked beans, navy, lima or pink
- 1 egg, beaten
- 1 large onion, chopped fine
- ½ cup cooked meat (any kind) chopped fine
- 1 teaspoon salt
- ½ teaspoon pepper
- ½ teaspoon ground red chili pepper
- Peanut oil for frying

Mash beans. Add rest of ingredients. Form into small balls. Coat lightly with flour. Sauté in hot peanut oil until crisp and brown.

◀ PEANUT BUTTER ▶

Roasted, shelled peanuts
Salt to taste **Peanut oil**

Run roasted, shelled, skinned peanuts through a meat grinder twice. If you want a creamier instead of crunchier peanut butter, run the peanuts through the grinder a third time. Add about 1 teaspoon of peanut oil to each cup of ground nuts, slowly creaming mixture as you add oil. Add a pinch of salt and cream again. You can also make peanut butter in a blender. Just run the peanuts, prepared the same way, through the blender, adding oil and salt to taste, until the peanut butter is the right consistency.

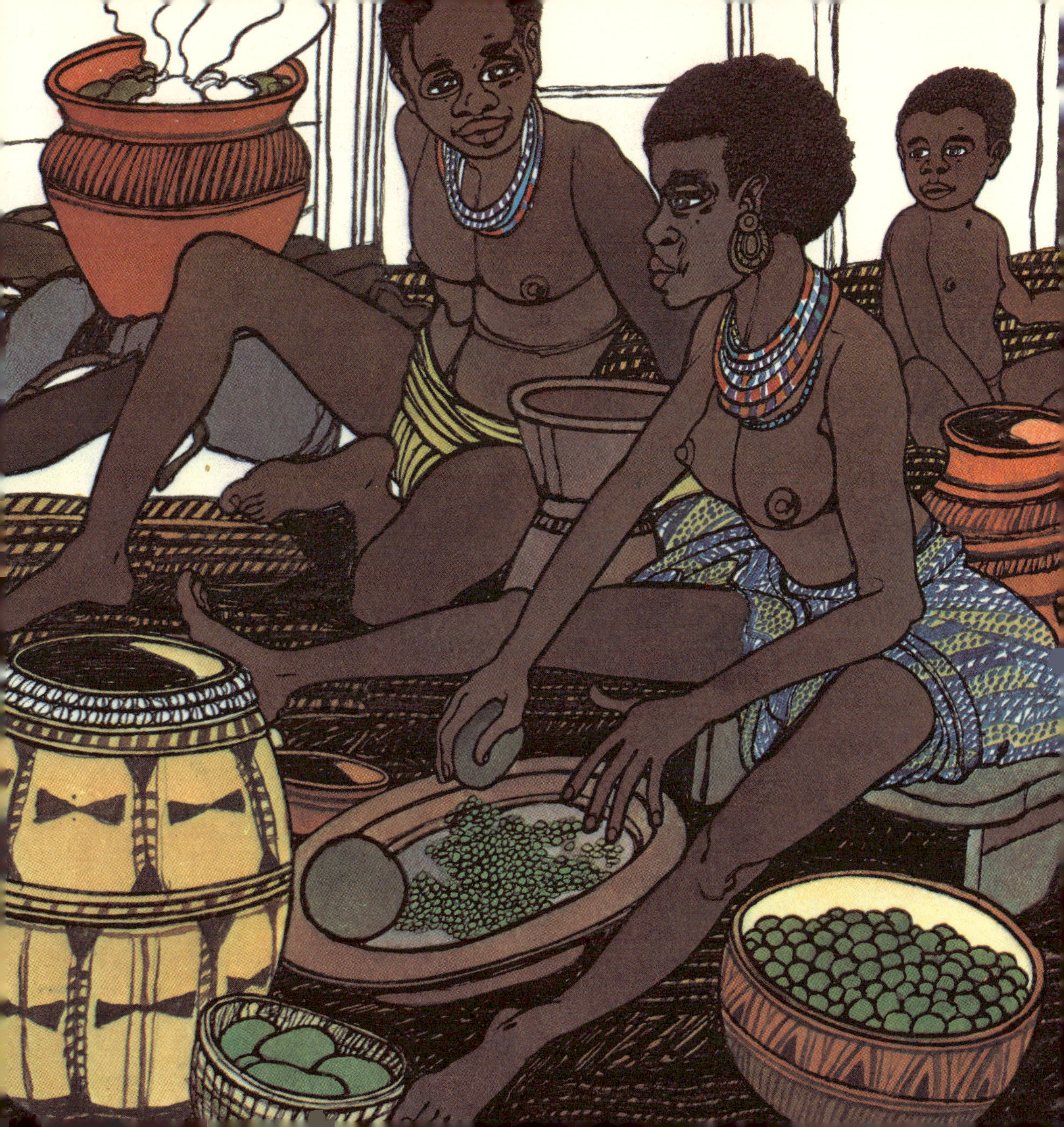

LAMB SNACKS

Rwanda

- 1 cup cooked lamb, coarse ground
- 2 tablespoons peanut oil
- ½ cup onion, minced
- 1 garlic clove, peeled, minced
- ¼ teaspoon ground ginger
- ¼ teaspoon ground coriander
- ½ teaspoon ground red chili peppers
- ½ teaspoon salt
- 2 eggs, beaten
- 3 tablespoons fine bread crumbs
- Peanut oil for frying

Sauté onions and garlic in oil until yellow. Add seasonings and stir. Add ground lamb and mix. Combine with eggs and crumbs in mixing bowl and mix well. Form into 1-inch balls. Fry in hot oil, turning and shaking pan until balls are brown on all sides.

HOT PEANUT SOUP

- 3 cups milk
- 2 tablespoons cornstarch
- 3 cups chicken broth
- 2 cups roasted peanuts, shelled, skinned and ground or mashed fine
- 2 tablespoons grated onion
- 2 tablespoons chopped parsley
- 2 teaspoons salt
- ¼ teaspoon pepper
- ⅛ teaspoon cayenne pepper
- ½ cup chopped chives for topping

Add cornstarch to milk and stir until smooth. Put into soup kettle with broth and all other ingredients except chives. Bring to a boil, stirring constantly. Turn down heat and simmer for 10 minutes, continuing to stir. Strain. Serve hot. Top with chives.

COLD AVOCADO SOUP

- 4 cups chicken broth
- 2 ripe avocados
- 4 teaspoons lime juice
- 1 teaspoon salt
- ½ teaspoon pepper
- 2 teaspoons minced chives

Peel and slice avocados, then mash. Add to broth and stir well. Add rest of ingredients, blend well and chill. Serve very cold.

RED BEAN SOUP

    2½ cups dried red kidney beans
    1½ quarts cold water
       2 beef shanks
       2 tablespoons peanut oil
       2 large onions, peeled, chopped
       1 tablespoon flour mixed with ½ cup cold water
    1½ tablespoons salt
       1 teaspoon black pepper
       2 large ripe tomatoes, chopped

Wash beans in cold water and drain. Put into deep soup pot with 1½ quarts cold water and beef shanks. Bring to a boil. Turn heat down, cover and simmer for 1½ hours. Remove beef shanks and set aside. Mash beans. Sauté onions until yellow. Add flour and water mixture and salt. Stir. Add tomatoes, and cook. Stir for a few minutes. Add onion mixture and shanks to beans. Cover and simmer for another ½ hour or until meat is tender. Remove shanks. Cut meat off bones and discard bones and fat. Cut meat into small pieces and return to soup. Serve hot.

◀ COLD SOUP ▶

Senegalese

- 3 tablespoons butter or margarine
- 2 medium-size onions, peeled, chopped
- 2 stalks celery, chopped
- 2 tablespoons flour
- 1 tablespoon curry powder
- Few drops sesame oil
- 2 cups cooked, minced chicken
- 1 quart chicken broth
- 1 cup light cream or half-and-half
- Salt and pepper to taste

Melt butter in frying pan. Add onions and celery. Cook over low heat until vegetables are tender. Stir in flour and curry powder. Add oil. Add 2 cups of broth. Cook and stir until well blended. Set aside. Put chicken and remaining 2 cups of broth into a blender and blend until smooth. Combine with vegetable mixture and cook for 5 minutes. Remove from fire. Chill. Just before serving, stir in cream.

SAMBHAR SOUP

(lentils or dried peas and vegetables)

- 1 cup lentils or split green peas, soaked overnight
- 1 large onion, peeled, chopped
- 1 bell pepper, chopped
- 2 potatoes, peeled, chopped
- 2 quarts water
- 3 teaspoons curry powder
- ½ cup tomato sauce
- 3 teaspoons salt
- ¼ teaspoon ground cumin
- ¼ teaspoon dry mustard
- Juice of 2 lemons
- Chopped Chinese parsley (fresh coriander leaves or cilantro)

Drain lentils. Put lentils, onions, peppers, potatoes and water into deep soup pot and bring to a boil. Stir well. Turn down heat, cover, and simmer until vegetables are soft. Put through a strainer or food mill, then back into pot. Add curry, tomato sauce, salt, cumin, mustard and lemon juice. Simmer for 10 minutes. Serve hot. Sprinkle with Chinese parsley.

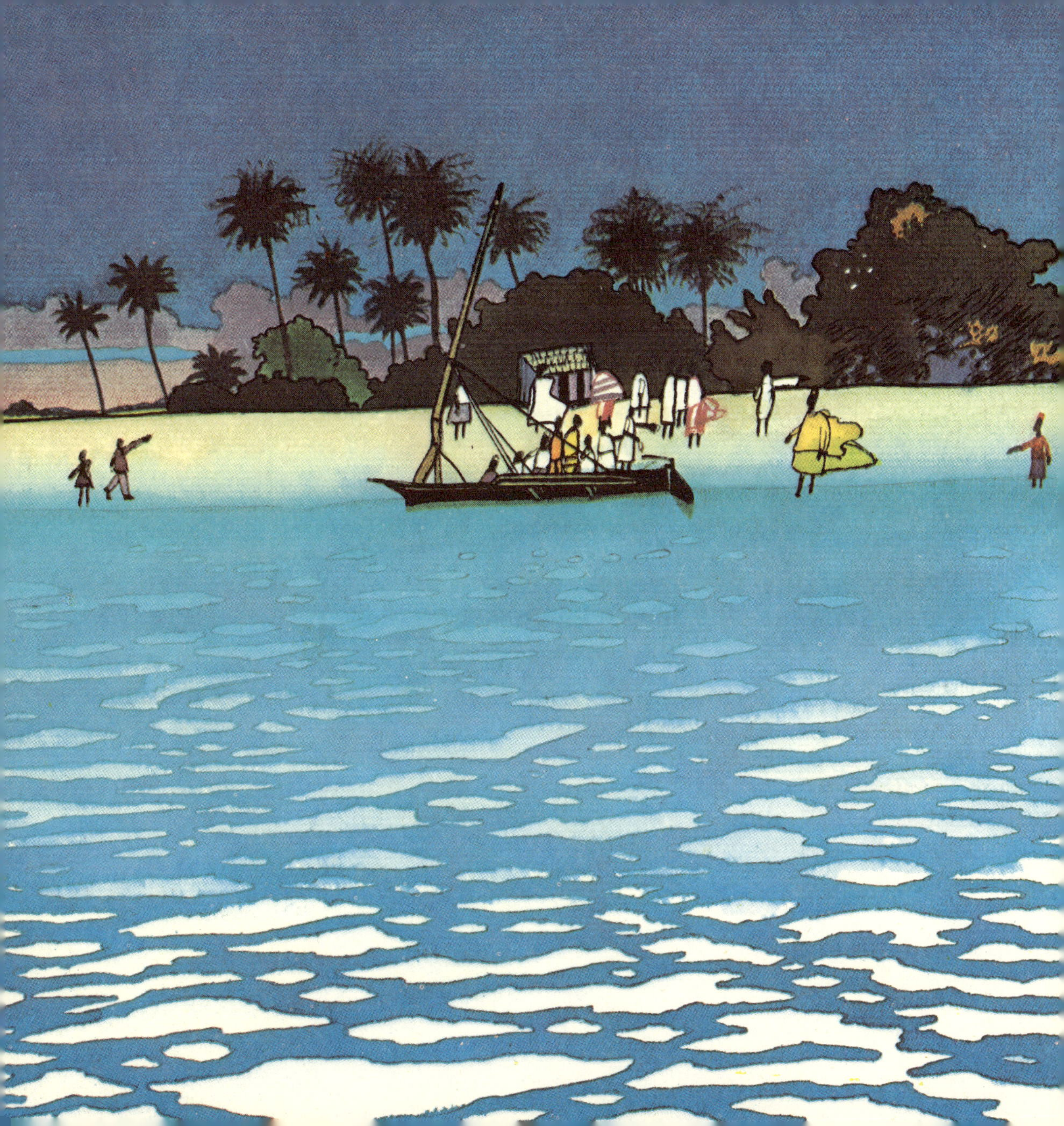

SALADE DES ILES

½ cup fresh coconut, grated
4 tomatoes, chopped fine
3 scallions, minced
½ green bell pepper, minced
1 small can white tuna fish, drained and chopped

MARINATE ABOVE INGREDIENTS FOR 4 HOURS IN THIS SAUCE:

½ cup olive oil
¼ cup vinegar
1 teaspoon salt
½ teaspoon pepper
1 tablespoon lemon juice

Add whole black olives and 2 sliced, hard-cooked eggs. Add 1 tablespoon of lemon juice just before serving. Serve on salad plate on bed of lettuce leaves.

◀ SALADE AFRICAINE ▶

Peel two ripe mangoes and cut into pieces. Mix with pieces of fresh pineapple, orange slices, shreds of coconut, sliced bananas and rings of papaya. Sprinkle with sugar. Add juice of 1 lemon and 1 tablespoon of white rum (optional). Serve very fresh.

◀ PAPAYA MOLD ▶

- 1 package lemon or lime gelatin
- 1 cup boiling water
- 1 cup apple juice
- 1 fresh papaya, peeled, seeded, chopped
- 1 minced green chili pepper, fresh or canned
- Sour cream

Add boiling water to gelatin and stir until gelatin is dissolved. Add apple juice. Stir. Put into mold and chill until partly set. Fold papaya and chili pepper into gelatin and chill until firm. Top with dollop of sour cream.

◀ PAPAYA SALAD ▶

Sierra Leone

Put peeled papaya slices, grapefruit sections, and chunks of peeled melon on plates. Sprinkle with sugar and fresh-grated coconut.

◀ CONGO AVOCADO ▶

(individual salads)

    1 peeled avocado (half per person)
    ½ cup flaked, cooked, cold white fish fillets
    1 to 2 tablespoons Pilli Pilli mayonnaise (page 97)
       Minced green onions
       Lettuce leaves

Mix fish and mayonnaise. Fill avocado half. Sprinkle with green onions. Serve on bed of lettuce leaves.

◀ AVOCADO SALAD ▶

Sierra Leone

Put seeded avocado halves (one per person) on plates. Sprinkle with salt, pepper and vinegar. Eat with a spoon.

AVOCADO SALAD

Nigerian

1 ripe avocado
   Juice of one lime
1 large ripe tomato, cut into wedges
   Lettuce leaves

DRESSING

¼ cup vinegar
¼ cup olive oil
¼ teaspoon pepper

Peel avocado, cut into slices and marinate in lime juice for half an hour. Remove slices. Make individual salads with lettuce leaves topped with avocado slices and tomato wedges. Put a few spoonsful of dressing on each salad.

◀ SHELLFISH SALAD ▶

    3 cups cold cooked prawns, shrimp or lobster, cut into chunks
    2 scallions, chopped fine
    2 tablespoons chopped fresh parsley
    Celery salt and pepper to taste
    2 eggs, hard-cooked
    2 limes, cut into wedges
    1 head lettuce or 1 bunch fresh spinach

Mix seafood with scallions, parsley and seasonings. Add enough mayonnaise to make it hold together. Serve on fresh lettuce or spinach leaves. Garnish with quartered hard-cooked eggs and wedges of lime.

MAYONNAISE

 2 egg yolks
 1 tablespoon vinegar
 1 teaspoon dry mustard
 1 teaspoon salt
 1 teaspoon sugar
 ¼ teaspoon paprika
 ½ teaspoon curry powder
 1½ cups salad oil
 3 tablespoons lemon juice

Put egg yolks, vinegar, mustard, salt, sugar, paprika and curry powder into a deep bowl and beat with electric beater until mixed. Add oil very slowly in thin stream, beating constantly until about ¼ cup of oil has been added and mixture starts to thicken, then add oil in larger amounts until all is used and mixture is thick. Blend in lemon juice.

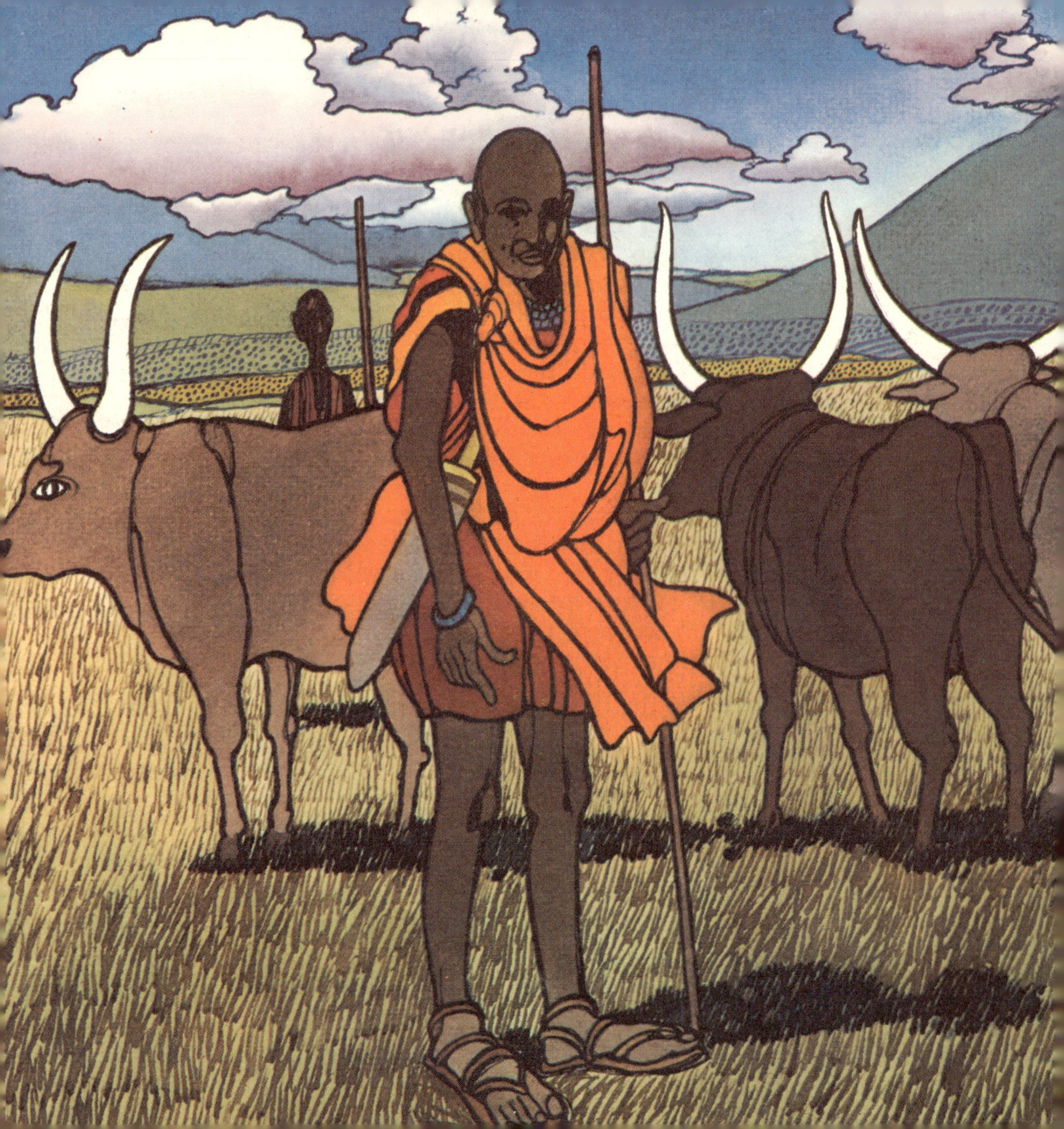

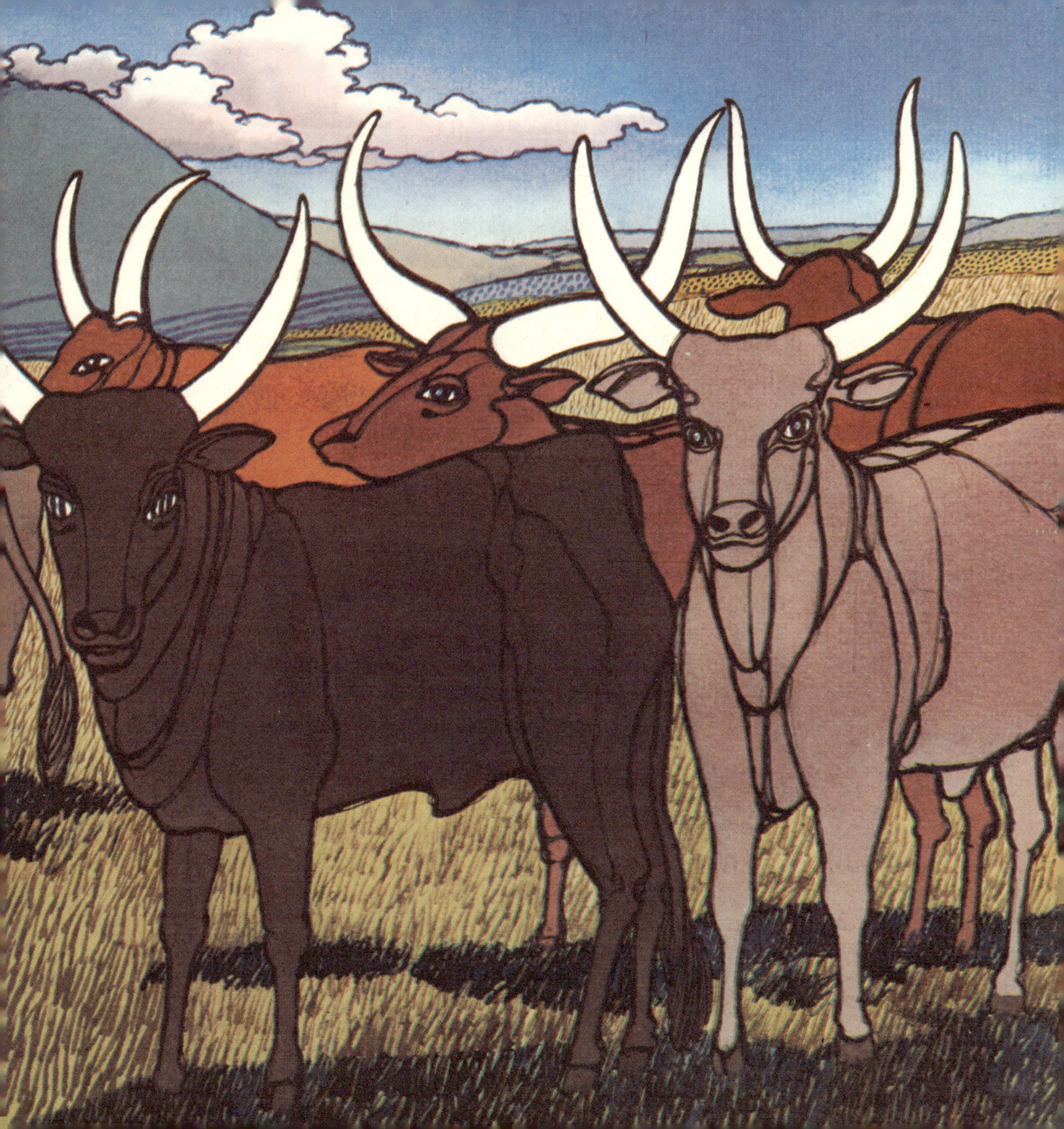

MEATS

Most African meat dishes are stews, and variety is achieved by the ingenious use of spices and peppers. Chunks of vegetables, portions of "mashes" or pieces of bread are dipped into the thin gravy. Some stews are prepared only for special occasions — weddings, funerals, the inauguration of chiefs, or the birth of twins.

SHOKO

(festival stew)

- 2 pounds boneless beef stew meat (tender cut), cubed
- ½ cup peanut oil
- 4 large tomatoes, chopped
- 6 medium onions, chopped very fine
- ½ teaspoon minced green chili peppers
- ½ teaspoon ground red chili pepper
- 1 teaspoon salt
- 1 cup water
- 1 pound fresh spinach leaves, washed and cut into small pieces

Brown meat in oil in heavy stewpot. Add water and simmer until tender. Add chili peppers, red pepper and salt. Add tomatoes and onions. Cook until vegetables are tender and very little water is left. Add spinach and cook until just tender.

COUSCOUS

1 cup couscous (packaged) or bulgar wheat, semolina or farina
2 cups boiling water
2 tablespoons butter
1 teaspoon salt
2 pounds boneless lamb, cubed
1 chicken, cut into pieces
6 tablespoons cooking oil
1 leek, washed and chopped
3 medium-size onions, chopped
2 green bell peppers, seeded and chopped
1 small can tomato sauce
1 teaspoon pepper
2 teaspoons salt
¼ teaspoon cayenne pepper
2 teaspoons chili powder
3 sweet potatoes, peeled, cut into chunks
4 carrots, peeled, cut into chunks
1 large can chick-peas, drained

Pour couscous slowly into boiling water while stirring. Add butter and salt. Cook until water is absorbed. Remove from heat, cover tightly, let stand 10 minutes. Put oil in heavy stewpot. Flour lamb and chicken pieces lightly and brown in hot oil. Add leek and onions and sauté until brown. Add water to cover, tomato sauce, pepper, salt, cayenne and chili powder. Put couscous in a colander or sieve that will fit into top of stewpot and still allow for fitting the cover on. Put colander over stewpot. Cover tightly. Bring to a boil. Turn down heat and simmer for ½ hour. Add green peppers, potatoes and carrots and simmer for another ½ hour, adding chick-peas for the last 5 minutes. Put couscous on large platter, and surround with drained meat and vegetables. Serve sauce in gravy boat.

CORN MEAL DUMPLINGS

1 cup corn meal
½ cup flour
1 teaspoon baking powder
½ teaspoon salt
2 eggs, beaten
½ cup milk
2 tablespoons melted butter
½ cup chopped parsley

Sift together corn meal, flour, baking powder and salt. Beat the eggs and add milk. Combine egg mixture and dry mixture. Stir in melted butter. Add parsley. Drop one tablespoonful at a time on top of boiling stew. Cover pot tightly and simmer for 15 minutes. Serve at once. Makes 8 dumplings.

GHANA STEW

2 pounds beef stew meat, cubed
6 medium-size onions, sliced
4 fresh tomatoes, chopped
1 teaspoon freshly ground black pepper
1½ teaspoons salt
4 tablespoons cooking oil
2 tablespoons flour
1 teaspoon grated nutmeg
Corn meal dumplings

Put meat in heavy stew pot. Sprinkle with salt. Add 1 sliced onion. Cover and cook over high heat for 10 minutes. Turn down heat and simmer for 1 hour. Put oil into frying pan and sauté remaining onions until yellow. Remove meat cubes from stew pot. Add pepper and nutmeg to flour and roll cubes in the seasoned flour. Sauté meat until brown. Put all ingredients into stew pot. Add tomatoes. Add water to cover. Simmer for 1 more hour. During last 15 minutes add dumplings. (Page 34)

◄ ZIGHINI ►

(spicy beef stew)

- 2 pounds stewing beef, bite-size pieces
- 1½ cubes (¾ cup) butter
- 2 large onions, chopped
- 1 large can tomatoes (2 pounds)
- ¼ teaspoon curry powder
- ⅛ teaspoon cayenne pepper
- 2 teaspoons chili powder

Sauté onion in butter. Add meat, tomatoes and seasonings. Simmer until tender.

◄ CHICHINGA ►

(skewered lamb or beef)

- 3 pounds leg of lamb or tender beef, cut in 1½-inch cubes
- 6 green peppers, washed, seeded, quartered
- 6 fresh tomatoes, washed, quartered
- 6 medium-size onions, quartered
- 1 cup cooking oil
- ½ cup vinegar
- 1 tablespoon salt
- ¼ teaspoon cayenne pepper

Place meat and vegetables close together on skewers. Brush with mixture of oil, vinegar and seasonings. Grill over hot fire, turning often.

◄ MCHUZI ►

(Tanzanian meat stew)

- 2 pounds beef stew meat, cut into bite-size pieces
- 1½ teaspoons salt
- 1 tablespoon lemon juice
- 1 large onion, peeled, chopped
- 2 tablespoons cooking oil
- 3 potatoes, peeled, cubed
- 3 carrots, scraped, sliced
- 1 teaspoon curry powder
- 1 cup beef stock

Put meat into stew pot with salt and lemon juice and just enough water to cover. Cook, covered, until tender. Sauté onion in oil until yellow. Add potatoes and carrots. Add curry powder and stir. Add onion and vegetable mixture to meat. Simmer covered, until vegetables are tender. Serve with Spicy Rice (page 81).

BIRIANI

(stew served at weddings and other celebrations)

- 2 pounds beef or lamb stew meat, bite-size pieces
- 3 large onions, sliced
- 1 clove garlic, minced
- 1 tablespoon chopped fresh ginger
- Seeds from 3 cardamom pods, crushed
- ½ teaspoon cinnamon
- ½ cup butter
- ½ cup cooking oil
- Juice from 6 limes
- 1 cup sour cream
- 1 teaspoon salt
- 2 cups rice, prepared as in Yellow Rice II recipe (page 82).

Put meat into heavy stewpot with cinnamon, garlic, ginger, cardamom seeds, sour cream, salt and lime juice. Add enough water to cover. Simmer until tender. Prepare rice. Melt half of the butter and fry onions until yellow. Add to meat. Add cooked rice in layer on top of meat. Melt rest of butter with oil and pour over top. Cover. Bake 20 minutes in 350° oven.

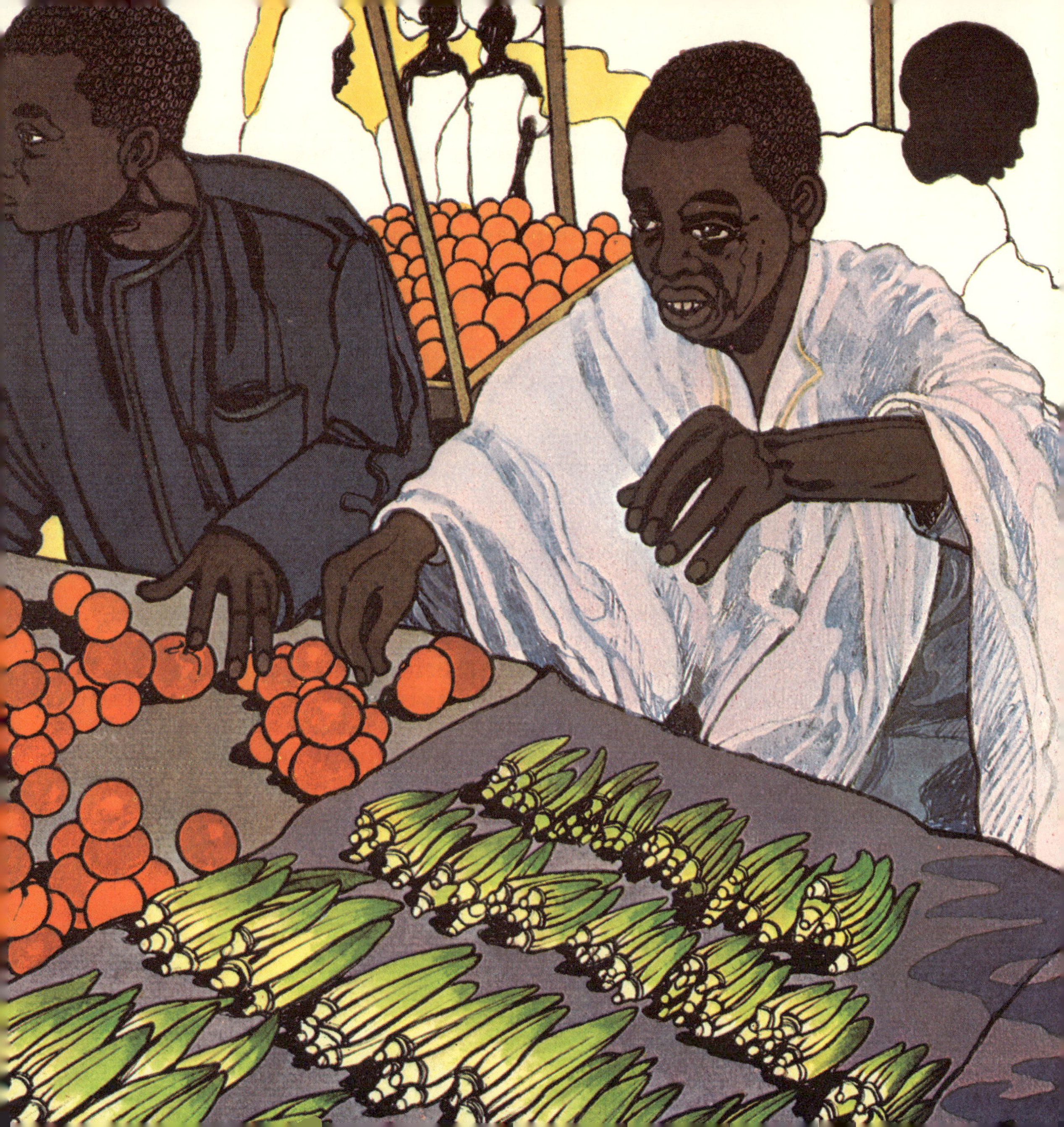

◀ GROUNDNUT STEW ▶

(beef and peanut stew)

2 pounds beef stew meat, cubed
2 tablespoons peanut oil
1 large onion, peeled, chopped
2 large tomatoes, peeled, chopped
2 cups water
½ green chili pepper, minced
½ teaspoon crushed red chili pepper
2 teaspoons salt
1 cup peanut butter
6 hard-cooked eggs

Brown beef in oil in heavy stew pot. Add 1 teaspoon of salt, half of the onions, tomatoes and chilies and 2 cups water. Cover and simmer for ½ hour. Mix the peanut butter with a cupful of juice from the stew and stir to a smooth paste. Add to stew. Add the rest of the onions, tomatoes and chilies and the seasonings. Cover and simmer for another half-hour or until meat is tender. Serve a whole hard-cooked egg with each bowlful of stew. Serve with one of the "mashes" (page 74-78).

BONDO GUMBO

(lamb and okra stew)

- 2 pounds lamb stew meat, cut into bite-size pieces, floured
- 3 tablespoons peanut oil
- 1 large onion, peeled, chopped
- ¾ cup tomato paste
- 2 teaspoons salt
- 2 cups water
- 1 (2-oz.) can pimentos
- ½ pound okra

Brown meat in hot oil in heavy stew pot. Add onion. Mix tomato paste with water and add. Add salt and pimentos. Cover and simmer for an hour or more until meat is tender. Prepare fresh okra by nipping off ends then cutting into 1-inch rounds. Add to stew and simmer covered until it is tender. Serve with steamed rice.

BANIA BAMIA

(Sudanese lamb and okra stew)

Follow the above recipe exactly except leave out the pimentos and add 1 clove peeled, minced garlic when you add the onion. Add ½ teaspoon cayenne pepper when you add the salt.

LAHAM MAA CURRY

(curried pork)

2 pounds pork loin, bite-size pieces
4 tablespoons cooking oil
2 green bell peppers, chopped
1 medium-size onion, chopped
2 tablespoons sherry
1 clove garlic, minced
1 teaspoon salt
½ teaspoon pepper
2 tablespoons curry powder
5 cups water

Fry pork in hot oil until well browned. Add remaining ingredients. Add 5 cups of water. Bring to a boil. Cover, turn heat down and simmer for about an hour. If gravy needs thickening make a paste of 2 tablespoons flour and ½ cup water and add while stirring.

KALE NYAMA

(angry hot meat)

4 lamb chops (shoulder chops will do)
1 small bottle ginger ale
1 teaspoon chili sauce
1 tablespoon chopped fresh mint leaves
　　or ½ teaspoon crushed dried mint leaves
1 teaspoon garlic salt
4 cloves

Put all ingredients except chops into bowl and mix well. Put chops in and marinate for 1 hour. Transfer chops and marinade to an oven-proof dish. Cover and bake 1 hour in moderate oven, basting several times. Add more ginger ale if chops get too dry.

◀ BRINJAL BURGERS ▶

2 pounds lean ground beef
1 thick slice white bread
1 teaspoon salt
1 teaspoon freshly ground black pepper
1 teaspoon dry mustard
1 egg, beaten
2 tablespoons catsup
½ clove garlic, minced fine
8 thin slices eggplant
8 thin slices onion
8 thick slices tomato
4 tablespoons cooking oil

Soak bread in milk and drain. Put into mixing bowl with beef, salt, pepper, mustard, egg and catsup. Mix thoroughly with hands. Shape into 8 patties. Peel and slice eggplant, onion and tomatoes. Heat oil. Sauté garlic, onion and eggplant for a few minutes. Remove and reserve. Fry patties to desired doneness. Serve with one onion, tomato and eggplant slice per patty.

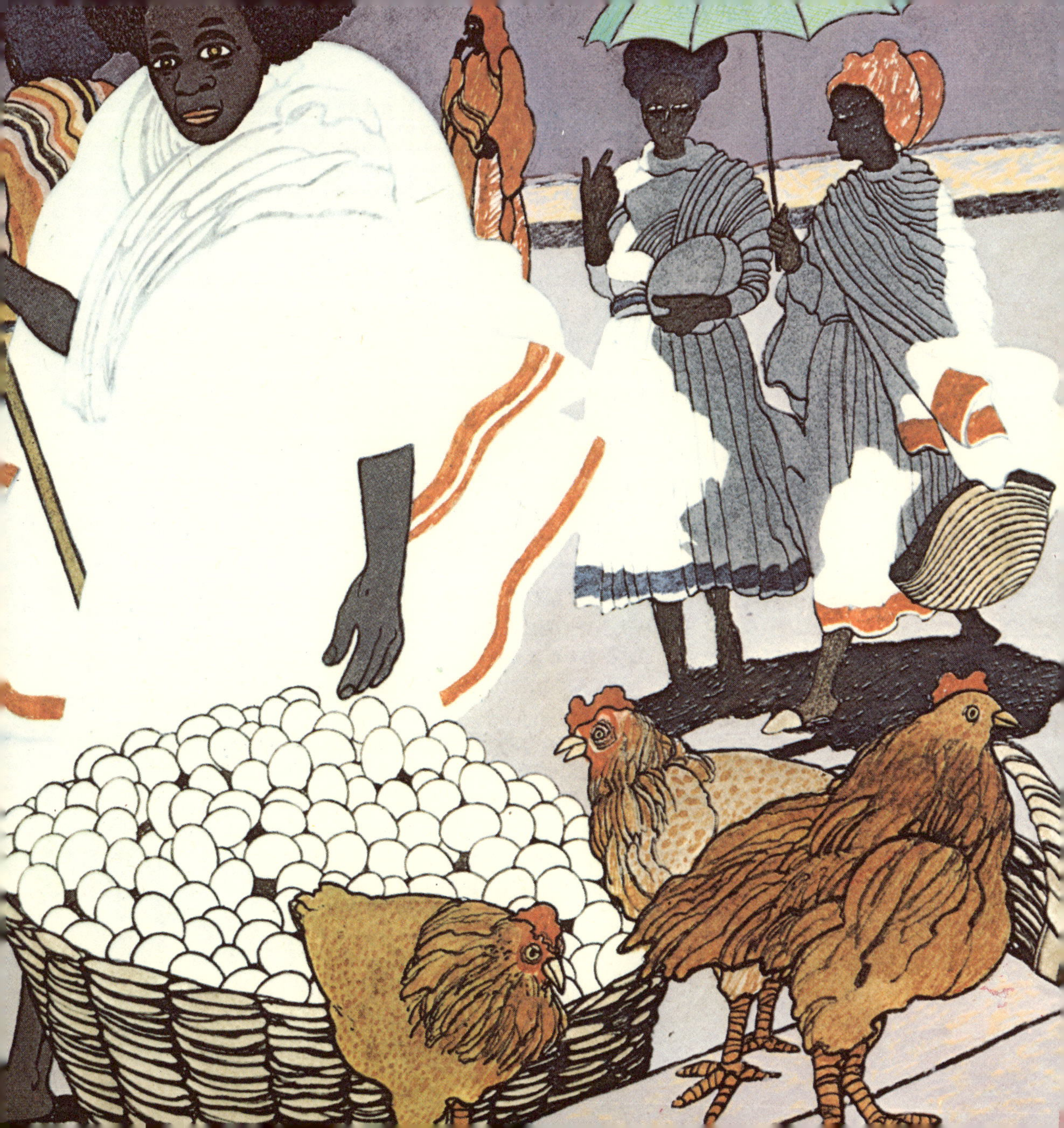

FORFAR BRIDIES

(meat pies)

½ pound tender beefsteak, trimmed, pounded and cut into strips ¼-inch wide
½ medium-size onion, minced
2 tablespoons beef suet, chopped fine
Salt and pepper to taste

Cut steak strips into short pieces. Add onion and seasonings. Moisten with a few drops of water and mix well.

DOUGH

1 cup flour
5 tablespoons margarine
½ teaspoon salt
4 tablespoons cold water

Sift flour and salt. Work in margarine with fork or fingertips. Add water to form stiff dough. Divide dough into two parts. Roll out each part into a thin oval. Place half the meat mixture on each. Sprinkle 1 tablespoon suet over each filling. Fold over and crimp edges of each pie. Bake on cookie sheet in 350° oven for ½ hour. For appetizers divide dough into 8 ovals and make 1 pie from each.

YASSA AU POULET

(chicken with lemon)

- 1 frying chicken, cut in serving pieces
- 8 tablespoons lemon juice
- 8 tablespoons vinegar
- ½ cup peanut oil
- 3 large onions, sliced
- 1 teaspoon salt
- ½ teaspoon pepper
- 1 large pimento or 1 (4-oz.) can pimentos, chopped

Put pieces of chicken, chopped pimento, salt and pepper into a bowl. Add lemon juice, vinegar and 2 tablespoons peanut oil. Soak chicken in the marinade for 10 minutes. Heat remaining oil in heavy pan and sauté chicken until brown. Remove and set aside. Sauté onion slices until yellow. Add the marinade, then the chicken. Add ½ cup water. Cover and cook until tender. This sauce can also be used for fish fillets.

GROUNDNUT STEW

(chicken and peanut stew)

1 stewing chicken, cut into serving pieces
2 cups water
1 green chili pepper, seeded and minced
    or 2 canned, peeled green chilies, chopped
1 cup roasted peanuts, shelled and skinned
    or ½ cup peanut butter (page 16).
1 teaspoon white pepper
2 teaspoons salt
½ teaspoon ground red chili pepper
2 large onions, sliced
4 eggs, hard-cooked, peeled, served whole
4 oranges, sliced
   Grated fresh coconut from 1 coconut
    or 1½ cups packaged coconut

Mash peanuts. Mix peanuts or peanut butter with water. Put in heavy stewpot. Add chicken, chili pepper, red and white peppers, salt and onions. Stew until tender. When serving, top the stew with hard-cooked eggs (1 per person). Place on platter with orange slices and coconut around it. Serve with yams and crusty bread.

◀ GROUNDNUT STEW ▶

Sierra Leone

- 1 chicken, cut into serving pieces
- 1 large onion, peeled, chopped
- 4 tablespoons peanut oil
- 2 mild green chili peppers, minced
- ½ cup unsalted, shelled, skinned, roasted peanuts, ground fine
- 2 cups hot water
- 2 teaspoons salt
- 2 tablespoons rice powder (rice flour) mixed with ¼ cup cold water
- 1 eggplant, peeled, cubed
- 1 squash (acorn or spaghetti) cut into 6 pieces

Heat oil in heavy stew pot. Brown chicken pieces. Add onions and chilies. Sauté for 5 minutes. Mix peanuts with hot water and add. Add salt. Simmer covered until chicken is tender. Remove chicken and set aside. Mix rice powder with cold water and add. Cook until stew is thickened. Return chicken to pot. While chicken is simmering, boil or steam eggplant until tender. Wash, cut, seed and brush the squash with oil, then bake for an hour or until tender. Serve stew with side dishes of vegetables.

Add:
- *chopped red/yellow peppers*
- *chopped celery*
- *lg can diced tomatoes*

◄ ETHIOPIAN HOT WAT ►

(chicken in hot sauce)

- 1 chicken, cut into serving pieces
- 2½ cups water
- 1 teaspoon salt
- Juice of 1 lemon
- 3 tablespoons butter or peanut oil
- 2 medium-size onions, peeled, chopped
- 2 cloves garlic, peeled, minced
- 4 tablespoons tomato paste
- ¼ teaspoon ground cardamom
- ½ teaspoon cayenne pepper
- 2 tablespoons chili powder
- 1 teaspoon finely-minced, peeled fresh ginger root
- 6 hard-cooked eggs, peeled and pierced with fork tines

Put water, salt and lemon juice into stew pot. Add chicken and simmer covered for 20 minutes. Remove chicken from stock and set both aside. Sauté onions and garlic in butter until tender and add to stock. Heat to boiling point. Add tomato paste, cardamom, cayenne, chili powder and ginger root and stir well. Add chicken. Simmer covered until chicken is tender. Add eggs to stew for the last ten minutes of simmering time. Serve one egg in each bowl of stew. Serve with Mock Enjera (page 67) or warm tortillas. If you want this dish hotter, add a small amount of Pilli Pilli sauce (page 97).

COCONUT CHICKEN

1 chicken, cut into serving pieces
1 whole onion stuck with 2 cloves
2 teaspoons salt
3 tablespoons oil
2 medium-size onions, sliced
3 tomatoes, peeled and chopped
1 clove garlic, minced
2 large bell peppers, seeded and cut into strips
2 teaspoons curry powder
1 teaspoon dried ground red chili pepper
2 cups coconut milk (page 120).
2 medium-size potatoes, peeled and sliced

Put chicken in stewpot with enough water to cover. Add whole onion stuck with cloves, and salt. Cover and simmer until nearly tender. Put oil in large frying pan. Sauté onions, tomatoes, garlic and peppers in oil until tender. Add curry powder and red pepper. When chicken is ready, lift out pieces and fry with the sautéed mixture for 5 minutes. Put sautéed ingredients into the stewpot with broth and add 1 cup coconut milk. Cover and simmer gently for 20 minutes. Add remaining coconut milk and potatoes and simmer another 20 minutes. When ready to serve, put chicken pieces on platter. Mash the vegetables in the liquid. Stir thoroughly and put sauce into a bowl. Serve in soup plates with plenty of crusty chunks of bread to dip into sauce.

AFRICAN GUMBO

(chicken and okra stew)

- 1 (3-4 lb.) chicken, cut into serving pieces, floured
- 3 tablespoons peanut oil
- 2 onions, peeled, chopped
- 4 tomatoes, peeled, chopped
- 1 quart chicken bouillon
- 1 teaspoon salt
- ½ teaspoon cayenne pepper
- 1 pound okra
- 1 tablespoon flour mixed with ¼ cup water

Brown chicken pieces in hot oil in stew pot. Add onions, tomatoes, bouillon, salt and cayenne. Simmer covered until chicken is tender. Wash okra, nip off ends, cut into rounds. Add okra and simmer covered until tender. Thicken with flour.

SHRIMP GUMBO

(shrimp and okra stew)

Substitute 2 pounds washed, shelled, de-veined shrimp or prawns for chicken and follow recipe for African Chicken Gumbo.

JOLOF RICE

Sierra Leone

1 smoked ham hock (weighing at least a pound)
2 cups chicken bouillon
2 cups beef bouillon
1 (3-4 lb.) chicken, cut into serving pieces
1 pound lean stewing beef
4 tablespoons peanut oil
2 medium-size onions, peeled, chopped
1 clove garlic, peeled, minced
2 large ripe tomatoes, peeled, chopped
2 tablespoons tomato paste
1 hot green chili (fresh or canned), minced
¼ teaspoon cayenne pepper
1½ cups raw long-grain rice
1 head cabbage, washed, cut into 8 pieces
1 eggplant, peeled, cut into chunks
1 small pumpkin, peeled, seeded, cut into chunks

Put ham hock in deep pot with chicken and beef bouillon and simmer covered for an hour. While hock is simmering, heat oil in heavy stew pot and brown chicken and beef. Remove from pot and reserve. Sauté onions and garlic for a few minutes. Add tomatoes, tomato paste, chilies, salt and cayenne. Stir and cook for 5 minutes. When ham hock is tender, remove it from bouillon, discard skin and bones and return pieces of ham to bouillon. Add bouillon, ham and beef to stew and simmer covered for an hour. Add chicken and simmer covered for another 15 minutes. Add rice. Stir well. Cover and simmer for another 20 minutes or until rice is cooked and chicken tender. Let stand for 15 minutes before serving so rice will absorb the liquid. Prepare vegetables by boiling or steaming and serve as side dishes.

◄ GROUNDNUT CHICKEN ►

¼ cup peanut oil
½ teaspoon cayenne pepper
3 pounds frying chicken pieces
1 cup peanut butter (page 16)
1 cup catsup

Heat oil until hot. Add cayenne and stir and heat for a few minutes. Brush chicken pieces with oil mixture. Mix remaining oil with peanut butter and catsup to make a thick basting sauce. Broil or grill chicken, basting frequently with the sauce. Takes about 45 minutes.

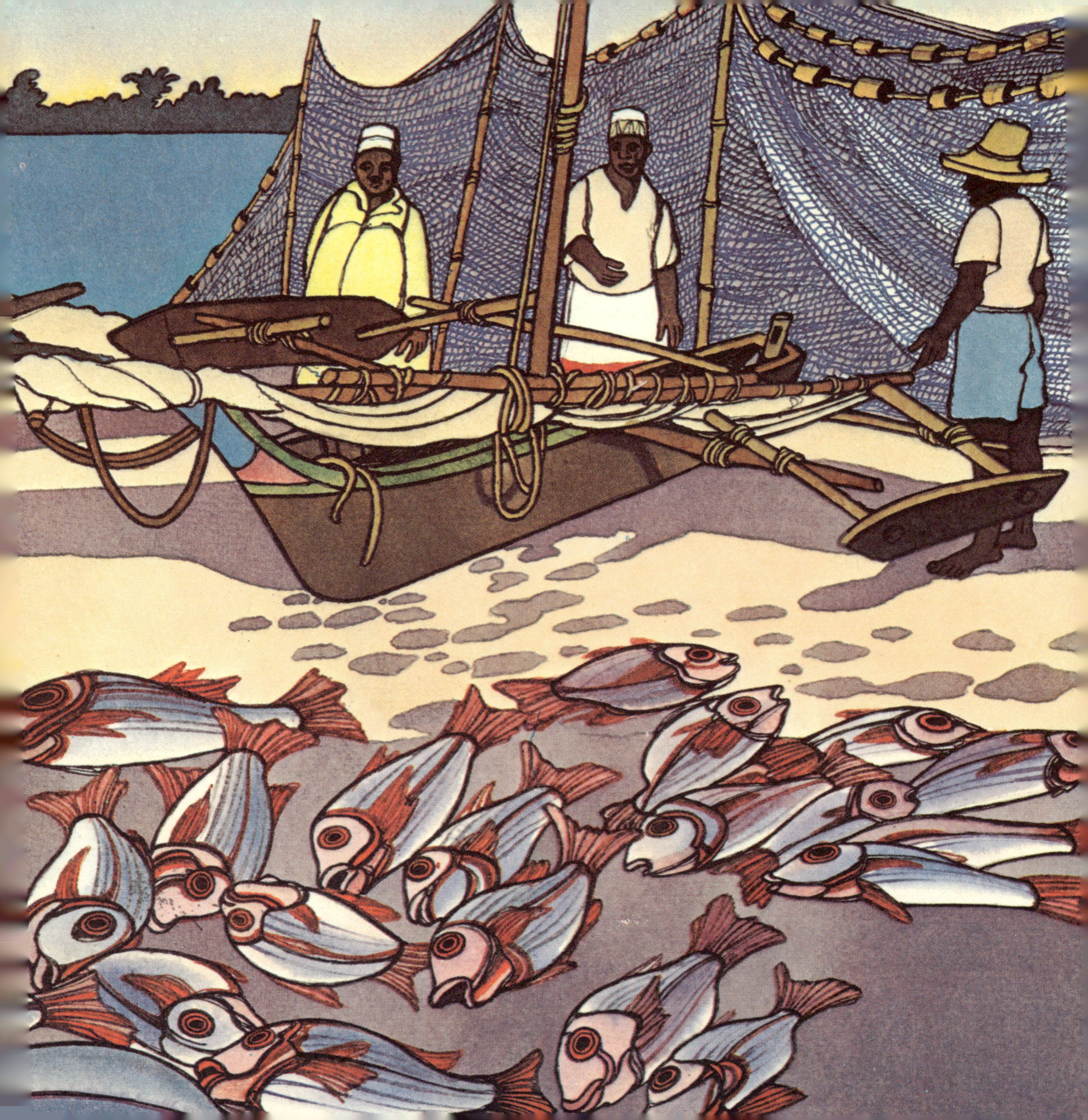

THIOU AU POISSON

(fish stew)

2 pounds boned fish, cut into bite-size pieces
3 medium-size white potatoes, peeled and cubed
2 medium-size sweet potatoes, peeled and cubed
½ medium-size head of cabbage, shredded
1 small can tomato paste (6-oz.) diluted with 1 cup water
1 medium-size onion, chopped
1 bay leaf
1 teaspoon salt
1 teaspoon pepper
1 cup olive oil for frying

In heavy stewpot, sauté white and sweet potatoes in ½ cup olive oil until brown. Remove potatoes and set aside. Add remaining oil. Sauté onions until yellow. Add tomato sauce, fish, salt, pepper and bay leaf. Add 3 cups water. Add cabbage. Bring to boil. Add potatoes. Cover, turn down heat and simmer until all ingredients are tender.

◀ NTOREWAFROE ▶

(eggplant and fish stew)

- 1 large eggplant, peeled, diced
- 1 medium-size onion, peeled, chopped
- 3 medium-size fresh tomatoes, peeled, chopped
- ½ teaspoon crushed, dried red pepper
- 1½ teaspoons salt
- 1 cup water
- 2 tablespoons peanut oil
- 1½ pounds fillet of sole, flounder or other white flat fish (seasoned with salt and paprika and brushed with oil)

Combine eggplant, onion, tomatoes, red pepper, salt and water in stewpot. Cover and simmer until vegetables are tender. Remove from fire and mash. Oil a shallow baking dish with peanut oil. Put half of mashed vegetables in dish. Make a layer of fish on top. Spread rest of the vegetables over fish. Bake uncovered in 350° oven for 20 minutes or more until fish is tender and flakes easily. Serve with steamed rice.

◀ SEAFOOD STEW ▶

4 tablespoons cooking oil
3 onions, chopped
3 tablespoons flour
2 cloves garlic, minced
3 teaspoons salt
1 teaspoon pepper
2 fresh green chili peppers, seeded and minced
　　or 1 (4-oz.) can peeled green chilies, chopped
2 quarts milk
2 pounds boned fish (2 or 3 kinds), cut into chunks
2 cups shrimp, shelled, cleaned, cut into chunks
1 toasted bread slice per person

In heavy stewpot sauté onions in oil until yellow. Add flour, stirring until smooth. Add garlic, salt, pepper and chili peppers. Add milk gradually, stirring until mixture boils. Add fish and shrimp. Bring to boil again. Turn down heat, cover and simmer until seafood is tender. Put one slice of toast in bottom of each soup bowl. Ladle stew over toast.

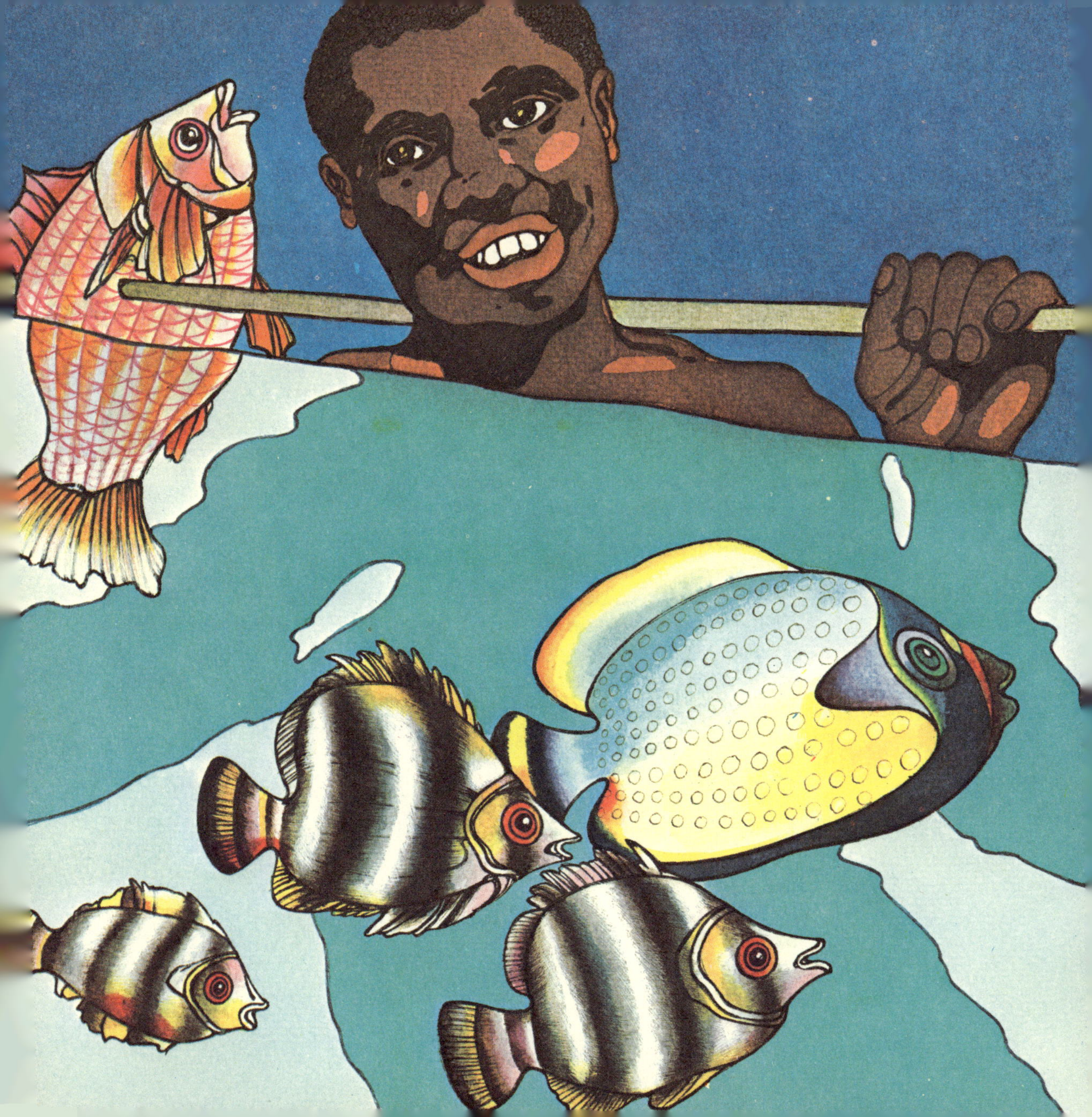

FISH CURRY

1 pound cod fish (or any firm, white fish)
1 large onion, peeled, chopped
2 tablespoons peanut oil
½ bell pepper, seeded, sliced
1½ cups tomato sauce

MARINADE

4 tablespoons rice vinegar (or white vinegar)
½ teaspoon ground red pepper
1 teaspoon curry powder
1 teaspoon sugar

Bone fish, then cut into serving pieces and lay in a shallow baking dish. Mix marinade and pour over fish. Turn and press pieces into marinade and let stand for an hour. Fry onions in hot oil until yellow. Add tomato sauce and green pepper slices. Simmer gently for 10 minutes. Add fish and marinade. Simmer for another 15 minutes or until fish is tender.

COCONUT SAUCE COD

- 2 pounds fresh cod (or defrosted frozen fillets)
- 2 cups coconut milk (page 120)
- ½ teaspoon salt
- ¼ teaspoon pepper
- 2 tablespoons chopped onion
- 1 teaspoon minced hot chili pepper
- 2 tablespoons butter
- 2 tablespoons flour
- 2 tablespoons chopped parsley

Bring coconut milk to a boil in large heavy saucepan. Add salt, pepper, onion and chili pepper. Reduce heat, add cod and poach gently until fish is tender and flakes easily when tested with a fork. Remove fish, transfer to a warm platter and keep in warm place. Turn heat up and reduce poaching liquid to about half. Reserve. Melt butter in heavy saucepan, add flour. Stir and cook until mixture is slightly browned. Gradually stir in the remaining poaching stock and continue stirring until it thickens. Pour over fish. Sprinkle with parsley. Serve with boiled rice.

FISH CAKES

Ivory Coast

- 2 pounds fish (boneless, white fillets)
- 2 eggs, beaten
- 1 clove garlic, peeled, minced
- 2 teaspoons salt
- ½ teaspoon ground red pepper
- 2 tablespoons cornstarch
- 1 cup peanut oil for frying

SAUCE

- 2 medium-size onions, peeled, chopped
- 2 cloves garlic, peeled, minced
- 4 large, fresh tomatoes, chopped
- 1 small can tomato paste (6-oz.)
- ½ teaspoon pepper

Make the sauce first. Combine all ingredients in order given. Mix well. Cook over low heat for 20 minutes. While sauce is cooking prepare cakes. Poach fish in water to cover until tender. Drain. Chop fine. Add eggs, garlic, salt, red pepper and cornstarch. Form into 3-inch-wide cakes. Heat oil. Fry cakes until golden brown on both sides. Drain on paper towels. Serve sauce with cakes.

LEMON COLD FISH

1½ pounds cod or other firm, white fish fillets
¼ cup peanut oil
1 clove garlic, minced
Juice of 2 lemons
1 teaspoon salt
¼ teaspoon pepper
2 teaspoons curry powder
¼ cup minced parsley
Lemon quarters and sprigs of parsley for garnish

Put oil into large skillet and sauté garlic in it for 3 minutes over medium heat. Put fish into pan. Mix lemon juice, salt, pepper, curry powder and parsley and pour over fish (adding a little water if needed). Cover pan. Turn down heat. Poach gently until fish flakes easily when tested with a fork. Let cool. Transfer fillets to a serving platter. Chill for half an hour before serving. Serve with lemon quarters and parsley sprigs.

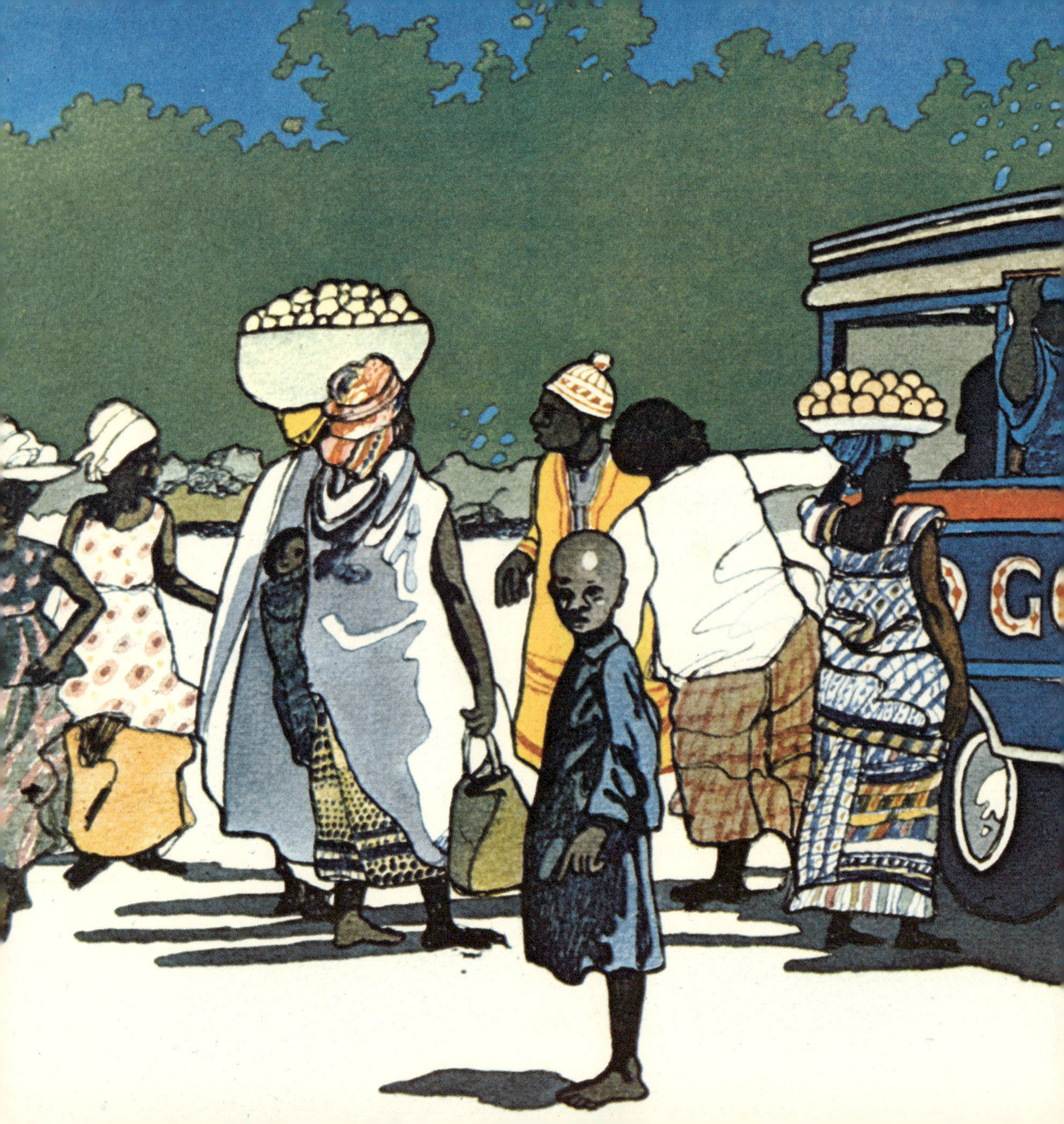

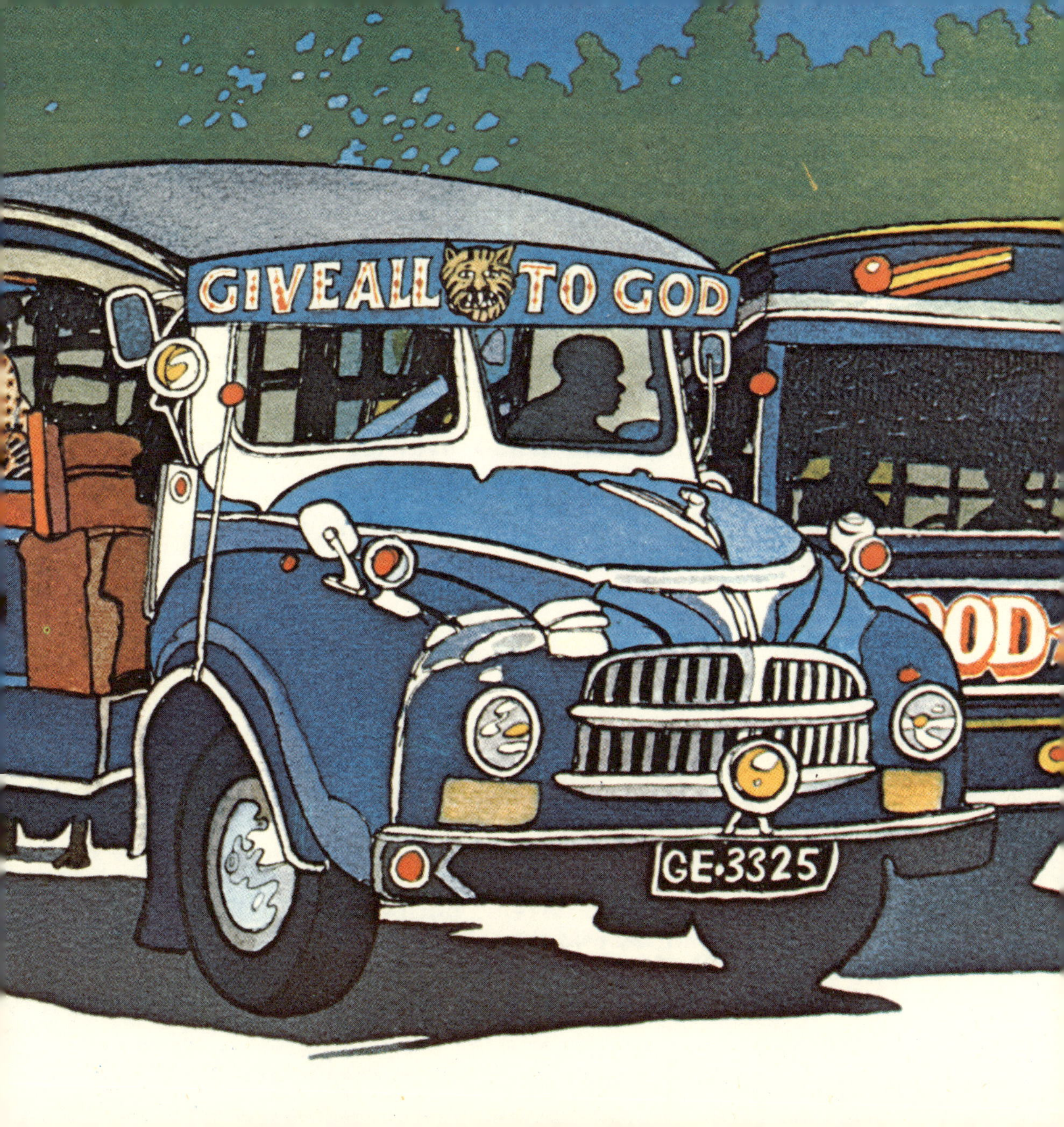
GIVE ALL TO GOD
GE·3325

◄ QUICK BREAD ►

- 4 cups sifted flour
- 2 teaspoons double-acting baking powder
- 1 teaspoon salt
- ½ to 1 cup milk

Sift flour, salt and baking powder together. Add enough milk to make a soft dough, but one that is firm enough to handle. Knead lightly for a few minutes on floured board. Shape into loaf. Put into greased bread tin. Bake in 350° oven for ¾ to 1 hour. Should be firm and golden brown.

◄ LIKOMA EASY DOUGH ►

- 1 pint lukewarm water
- 1 teaspoon salt
- 2 teaspoons sugar
- 1 tablespoon yeast (dry)
- 6 cups flour (approximately)

Put water, salt, sugar, yeast and 1 heaping tablespoon flour in bowl. Do not stir. Cover and let rise in warm place for 15 minutes. Stir it up and add 5 cups flour, stirring and mixing until well-mixed. Cover and let rise 15 minutes. Put dough on floured board and knead for 5 minutes adding enough flour to keep it from sticking and to make it firm. Shape into 2 loaves. Put in greased medium-size tins. Let rise until dough doubles in bulk. Bake in 400° oven for 30 minutes.

ENJERA

Enjera, the thin pancake-like bread served with Ethiopian wats (stews), is made with flour made from a grain called teff. Since this flour is unavailable we make a "mock" enjera which is something like a buckwheat crêpe.

- ½ cup buckwheat pancake mix
  (natural stone-ground buckwheat flour is best)
- 1 cup buttermilk
- 3 tablespoons flour
- 1 egg, beaten
- Cooking oil

Put pancake mix in bowl and add other ingredients one at a time, beating them into batter until smooth. Or put ingredients into a blender and blend for 20 seconds. Heat 9-inch frying pan until very hot. Beat 1 tablespoon cooking oil into batter. Brush frying pan with oil. Pour about 3 tablespoons of batter into pan and tip and turn pan to swirl batter around until it covers bottom of pan evenly and thinly. Cook until crêpe is set on bottom, then turn with spatula and cook for about a minute on the other side. Crêpes should be light brown. Makes 8. Serve in a basket as an accompaniment to stews. Flour tortillas are a good substitute for enjera and are available in most U.S. grocery stores.

CORN CAKES

1 cup corn meal (white)
1 tablespoon sugar
1 teaspoon salt
1 cup boiling water
½ cup milk
1 cup sifted flour
4 teaspoons baking powder
1 egg, beaten
Peanut oil for frying

Put cornmeal, sugar and salt into a bowl. Pour in boiling water, stirring and mixing as you pour. Set aside until the cornmeal swells and mixture cools. Add milk and stir. Add flour and baking powder and stir. Add egg and beat until all ingredients are blended. Drop the batter from a tablespoon into hot, lightly greased frying pan. Brown cakes on one side, then turn and brown them on the other. Makes 2 dozen (2-3 inch) cakes.

◄ CORN FRITTERS ►

1 cup boiled corn, cut from the cob
2 eggs, lightly beaten
6 tablespoons flour
½ teaspoon baking powder
¼ teaspoon salt
⅛ teaspoon pepper
⅛ teaspoon nutmeg
Peanut oil for frying

Mash corn thoroughly. Add beaten eggs, flour, baking powder and seasonings and stir until well blended. Heat oil in frying pan. Drop the batter from a tablespoon. Fry the fritters on one side until brown, then turn and brown them on the other.

BANANA BREAD

  2 bananas, mashed
½ cup sugar
¼ pound butter or margarine
  2 eggs, separated
  1 tablespoon milk
  2 cups sifted flour
  1 teaspoon salt
  1 teaspoon soda
  1 teaspoon baking powder
½ cup chopped peanuts

Mash bananas and set aside. Cream sugar and butter until light. Beat egg yolks and add. Beat well. Stir in bananas and milk. Sift dry ingredients together and beat into creamed mixture. Add peanuts. Beat egg whites until stiff and fold into batter. Put into greased bread tin and bake at 350° for 1 hour.

◀ RICE BREAD ▶

Sierra Leone

- ¾ cup rice flour (obtainable in Oriental markets, sometimes called rice powder)
- ⅓ cup sugar
- 1 banana, mashed to a paste
- ¼ teaspoon nutmeg
- Pinch of soda
- ½ cup raisins
- ½ cup currants
- 1 teaspoon grated orange peel
- 1 teaspoon grated lemon peel

Mix banana and sugar. Sift dry ingredients together. Combine and beat well. Shake raisins and currants in paper bag with 2 tablespoons of flour until coated, then add. Spread dough in thin, even layer in a 9-inch round cake pan. Sprinkle with grated peels. Bake at 350° for 40 minutes until quite brown. Makes a crusty, chewy inch-high loaf of bread.

PEANUT MUFFINS

- ½ cup butter or margarine
- ¼ cup sugar
- 2 eggs, beaten
- ½ cup milk
- 1½ cups, flour
- 1 teaspoon baking powder
- ¼ teaspoon salt
- ¾ cup minced, roasted, skinned, unsalted peanuts

Cream butter or margarine and sugar until light. Combine eggs and milk and add to creamed mixture. Sift flour, baking powder and salt and add. Mix until all ingredients are blended. Add ½ cup peanuts. Fill greased muffin tins about ⅓ full. Sprinkle tops of muffins with remaining peanuts. Bake at 400° for 12 minutes. Serve hot with honey. Makes 12 large or 18 medium muffins.

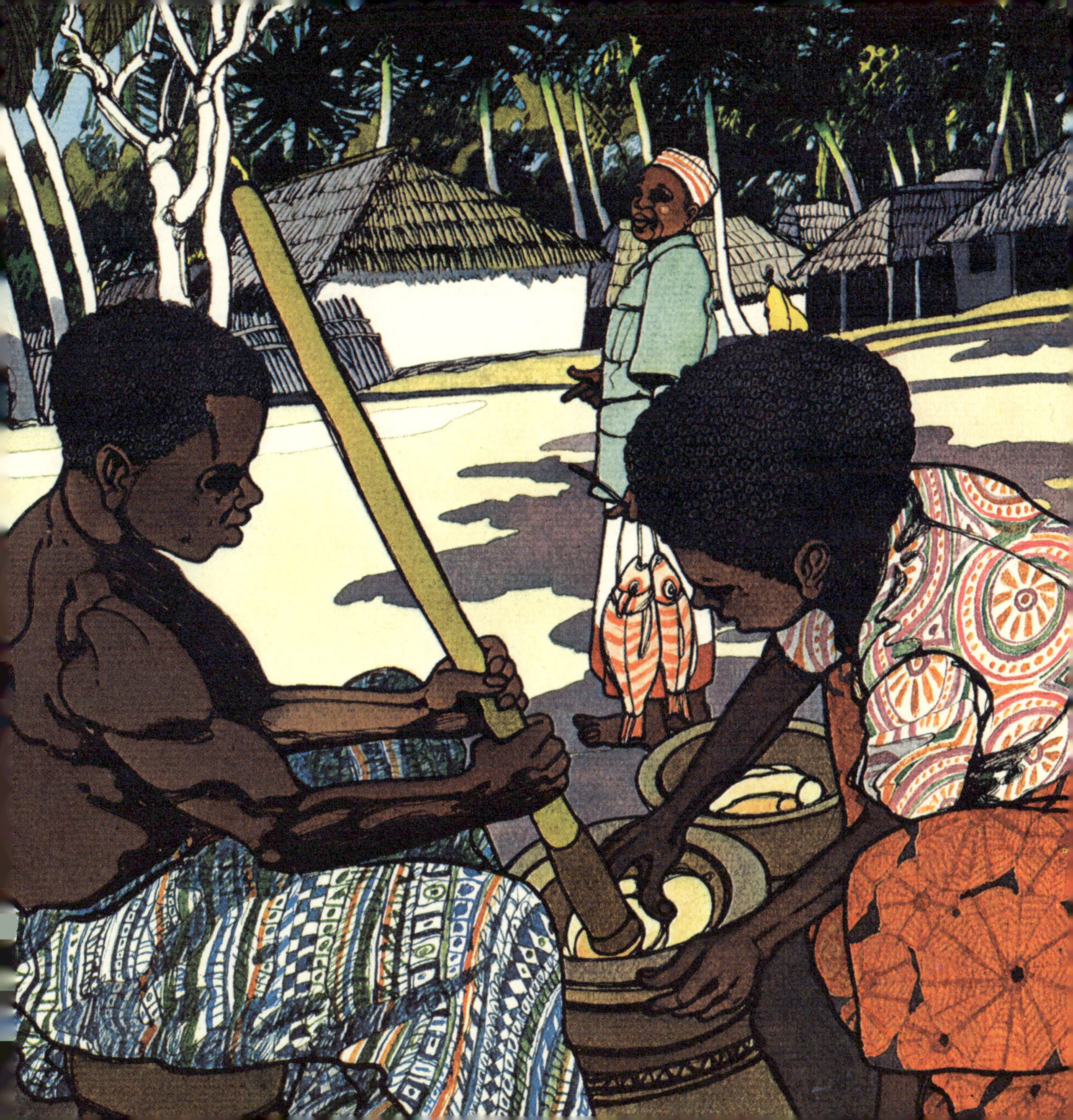

MASHES

Most tropical African countries have a favorite "mash," a bland, starchy dish to serve with traditional hot, spicy stews. The "mashes" are made from root vegetables such as cassava, yams or potatoes, fruits such as plantains or green bananas, or cornmeal.

Preparation of some of these national dishes is complicated and some ingredients (such as cassava, which is widely used in West Africa) are not available everywhere. Crusty breads, dumplings, rice or tortillas may be substituted, but for those who want to approximate some of the "mashes," recipes follow:

FUFU

(Americanized version of West African cassava Fufu)

Peel and boil 8 white potatoes until tender. Drain, mash and add ½ tablespoon of rice flour (can be bought in Oriental markets) per potato. Sift flour in, beating all the time with a wooden spoon. Continue to beat until mixture is smooth. Serve in a mound in a warm dish.

Yam or Sweet Potato Fufu can be made the same way, except it is better to steam, not boil, these vegetables until tender. Let them cool slightly before mashing and beating.

MATOKE

Uganda

Peel one plantain per person and cut lengthwise into halves. Lay on rack in a steamer. Heat water to the boiling point, then cover and steam until plantains are soft but not mushy. Lift them out, put into a bowl and mash. Add a little salt and beat with a wooden spoon or paddle until smooth, adding a little boiling water from the steamer as you mash to make the mixture the consistency of very thick mashed potatoes.

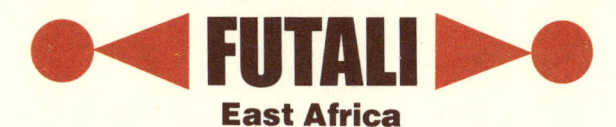

FUTALI

East Africa

Peel 1 large sweet potato per person, cut into chunks and boil in water to cover until tender. Drain. Add ½ cup per potato of shelled, roasted, unsalted peanuts ground fine, and mash. Beat with heavy wooden spoon until smooth. Add a little salt if you wish. Serve hot.

IRIO

Kenya

Peel, boil and mash 6 white potatoes. Mix with 1 tablespoon finely chopped sorrel leaves or watercress. Add 1 cup cooked green peas and 1 cup cooked white corn. Season with salt, pepper and butter and mash all together thoroughly. Serve hot.

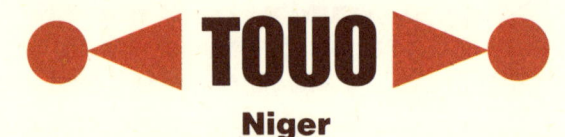

TOUO

Niger

Bring 2 cups of water to a boil. Add ½ teaspoon of salt. Mix 1 cup of white corn meal with 1 cup of cold water to form a paste. Stir this paste slowly into the boiling water. Turn heat down and simmer and stir for about 10 minutes or until consistency of mush. Add a lump of butter if you wish.

UGALI

East Africa

Add 1½ cups corn meal slowly to 2 cups boiling water, stirring constantly. Add a pinch of salt. Cook and stir until consistency of very stiff porridge. To eat, take a portion, roll it into a sphere, make an indentation with the back of a tablespoon for the stew.

BEAN UGALI

Tanzania

Rinse 1 cup dry white beans with cold water. Cook covered in 3 cups water until soft. Put them through a coarse sieve to extract skins. Peel and mince 1 onion and fry in 1 tablespoon peanut oil until yellow. Add a tablespoon of flour and brown. Add ½ cup hot water slowly, stirring until mixture boils. Add ½ teaspoon salt, 2 tablespoons ground peanuts and the beans. Cook and stir for 5 minutes.

◀ WATER BREAD ▶

(To Serve With Fish)

⅓ of a loaf of white bread and 1 medium-size onion (per person), butter, salt, pepper and boiling water. Slice the bread and butter it generously on one side. Chop the onions fine. Put the bread, one slice at a time, into a large bowl. Cover each slice with a layer of onions before adding the next slice, and sprinkle each layer with lots of salt and pepper. Take the kettle of boiling water in your left hand and a large sharp-edged spoon in your right. Pour the boiling water into the bowl a little at a time while chopping and turning the mixture with the spoon. Keep pouring and chopping until the mixture is the consistency of mashed potatoes. Serve immediately.

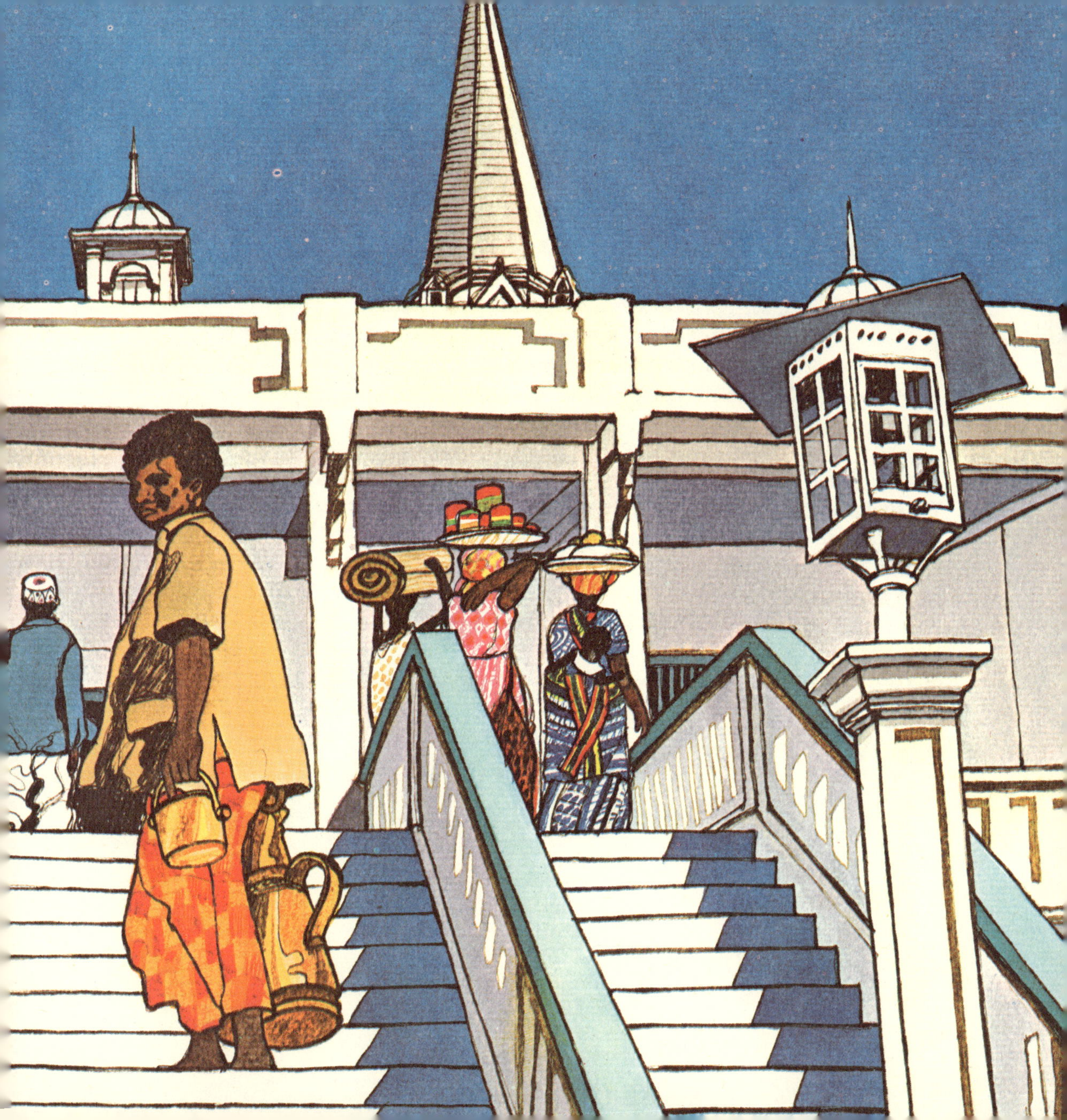

SAVORY RICE

1½ cups long grain rice
4 tablespoons butter
4 tablespoons oil
2 medium-size onions, chopped
1 green chili pepper, seeded and chopped
3 cups chicken broth
2 teaspoons salt
1 teaspoon pepper

Wash rice thoroughly and drain. Heat 2 tablespoons butter and 2 tablespoons oil in heavy casserole and sauté rice until light brown, stirring constantly. Sauté onions and chili pepper in remaining butter and oil until tender. Add to rice. Add salt, pepper and broth and mix well. Cover and bake in 350° oven 30 to 40 minutes, or until broth is absorbed and rice slightly brown.

Note: In all rice recipes allow ⅓ cup uncooked rice per person.

STEAMED RICE

    1 cup long grain rice
    2 tablespoons oil
    2 cups chicken bouillon
    ½ teaspoon salt

Put rice into a strainer and rinse under cold water. Shake off excess water. Sauté rice in oil for a few minutes. Put into a casserole. Add salt and bouillon. Bring to a boil. Cover, turn heat down and simmer for about 20 minutes or until rice absorbs all liquid.

SPICY RICE

    1½ cups coconut milk (page 120)
    ½ cup rice
    2 whole cloves
    1 stick cinnamon

Heat milk. Add rest of ingredients. Cook covered over low heat for 20 to 30 minutes until rice absorbs liquid. Remove cloves and cinnamon stick. Serve with curried meat dishes.

YELLOW RICE I

- 1 cup rice
- 2 cups water
- 1 tablespoon butter
- ½ cup brown sugar
- 1½ teaspoons ground or grated turmeric
- 1½ teaspoons salt
- ½ cup seedless golden raisins (optional)
- ¼ teaspoon cinnamon

In heavy saucepan mix rice with other ingredients in above order. Cover. Bring to a boil. Stir. Reduce heat to low. Cover and cook until rice is tender (about 25 minutes).

YELLOW RICE II

2 cups rice
4 tablespoons cooking oil
4 cups chicken broth
2 teaspoons salt
¼ teaspoon ground saffron

Wash rice in cold water and drain. Sauté in oil until light brown. Add remaining ingredients. Bake in covered casserole in 350° oven 30 to 40 minutes.

RICE CAKES

1 cup cooked rice
1 tablespoon fried onions
½ teaspoon curry powder
1 egg
3 tablespoons flour
Peanut oil for frying

Mix all ingredients together. Drop by tablespoonsful into hot oil and fry as you would pancakes until brown on both sides. Can be eaten warm or cold.

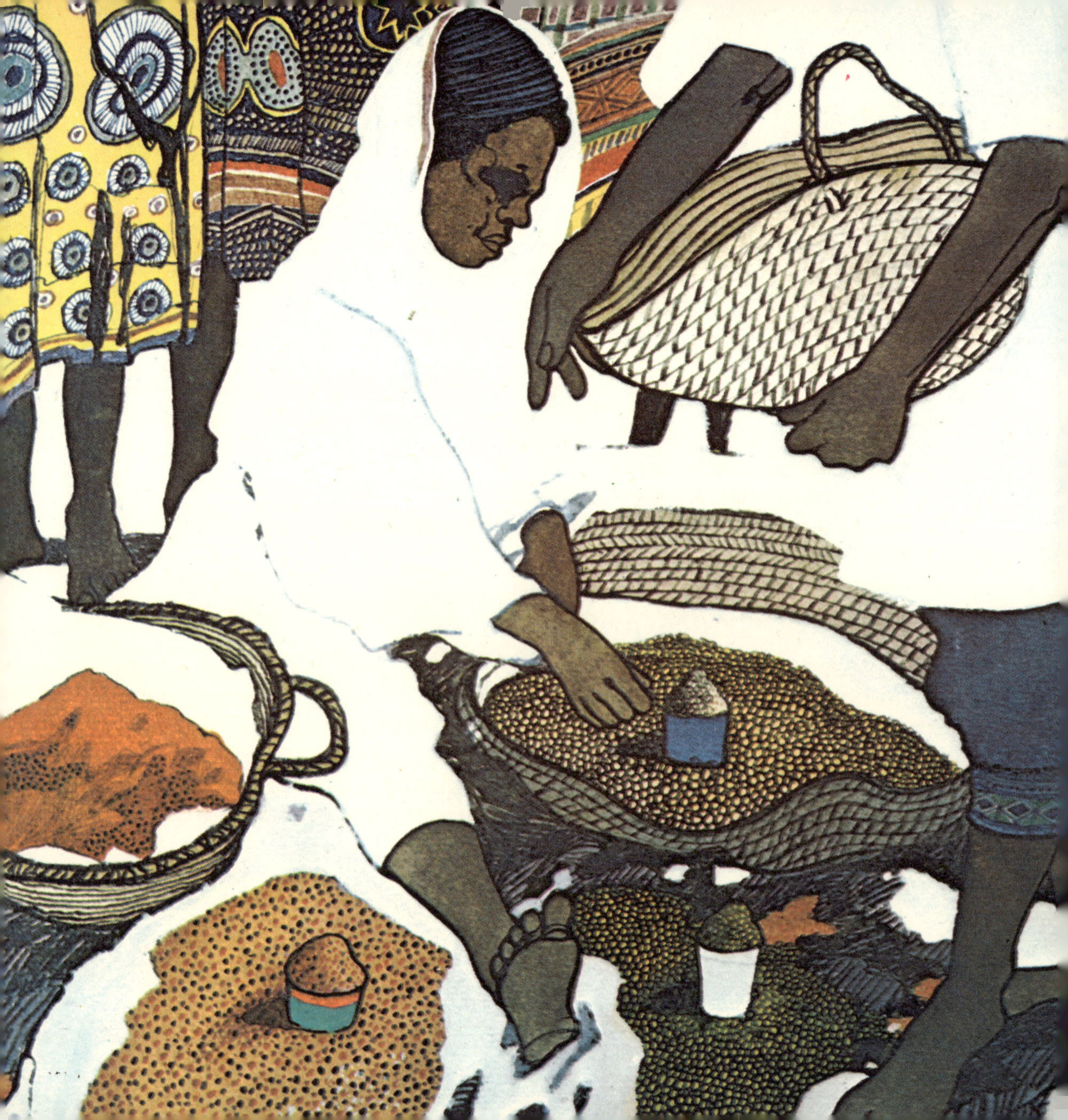

◀ MAIS DE MOMBASA ▶

(corn dish)

- 1 tablespoon butter
- 1 medium-size onion, chopped
- 1 clove garlic, minced
- 4 cups whole kernel corn (fresh, canned or frozen)
- 1 small tomato, chopped
- 1 (2-oz.) can pimentos, chopped
- 2 teaspoons cornstarch
- 1½ cups coconut milk (page 120)
- ¼ teaspoon ground turmeric or curry powder
- 1 teaspoon salt
- Juice of half a lemon
- Few sprigs of parsley (Chinese if available) chopped fine

Melt butter in heavy saucepan. Add onion and garlic and sauté until yellow. Add corn. Put cornstarch in 1 cup of coconut milk, stirring well until dissolved, and add. Add turmeric, tomato, pimentos and salt. Cook uncovered, stirring often, until juice is absorbed. Remove from fire. Add remaining coconut milk and lemon juice. Stir. Top with parsley. Serve as vegetable accompaniment to main dish.

◄ BURUNDI BEANS ►

- ½ pound black-eyed peas, navy or pink beans
- 2 quarts cold water
- ¼ cup peanut oil
- 1 large onion, peeled, chopped
- 1 clove garlic, minced
- 1½ teaspoons salt
- 1 teaspoon crushed, dried red chili peppers

Wash peas in cold water and drain. Put into deep kettle with water. Bring to a boil, then turn heat down and simmer for 30 to 45 minutes or until peas are tender. Heat oil in large frying pan. Add onions and garlic and sauté until transparent. Drain peas and run through a foodmill or coarse sieve. Add peas to onions. Add salt and red pepper. Cook and stir for 5 minutes. This dish can be served hot or cold.

◄ CHAD SQUASH ►

- 6 summer squash or yellow crook-neck squash
- ½ cup water
- ½ teaspoon salt
- ½ cup minced peanuts
- 1 tablespoon butter or margarine
- 1 teaspoon sugar

Cut stems from squash but do not peel. Cook in water to cover until tender. Drain well and mash. Add salt, butter and sugar. Put into a baking dish and bake at 325° uncovered for about 10 minutes. Serve hot.

◀ DUN DUN ▶

(fried yam slices)

- 6 medium-size yams or sweet potatoes, peeled and cut into ½-inch slices
- Water to cover
- 1 teaspoon salt
- 1 cup flour, seasoned with 1 teaspoon each of salt and pepper
- 2 eggs, beaten lightly and mixed with 2 tablespoons water
- 6 small scallions, chopped
- Oil for frying

Boil slices in salted water until tender. Drain and let dry. Put seasoned flour into one bowl and egg mixture into another. Dip slices first in flour, then in egg, then in flour again. Fry until golden brown on both sides and serve piping hot sprinkled with scallions.

◀ NDIWO ▶

(tomato-egg dish)

- 6 hard-cooked eggs, peeled and pierced once with fork tines
- 3 medium-size onions, chopped
- 4 large tomatoes, peeled and chopped
- ½ cup peanut oil
- 1 teaspoon salt
- 1 tablespoon curry powder
- ½ cup hot water

Place diced tomatoes in hot oil in frying pan. Add onions. Sauté until the mixture is soft. Add curry and salt. Mix well. Add whole hard-cooked eggs (piercing makes them absorb sauce) and drench in mixture. Add hot water. Simmer 15 minutes.

◀ MCHICHA ▶

(spinach)

- 1 pound fresh spinach
- ½ large onion, chopped
- 1 large fresh tomato, chopped
- 2 tablespoons cooking oil
- ½ teaspoon salt
- ½ teaspoon pepper
- 1 tablespoon curry powder

Wash spinach and steam in a saucepan for a few minutes using only the water clinging to the leaves after washing. Sauté onion and tomato in oil until tender. Add cooked spinach and seasonings. Stir well. Serve hot.

BAJIAS

(potato balls)

- 2 large potatoes, peeled, boiled
- ½ hot green chili pepper, minced
- 1 teaspoon minced Chinese parsley (fresh coriander leaves or cilantro)
- 1 teaspoon salt
- Pinch of ground ginger
- Peanut oil for deep frying

BATTER

- 1 tablespoon flour
- Pinch of salt
- Water to make a medium-thick paste

Mash potatoes. Add chili pepper, parsley, salt and ginger. Form into 2-inch balls. Roll balls around in batter to coat evenly. Deep fry in hot oil until golden brown. Makes 8.

MCHICHA

East Africa

1 pound fresh spinach
½ large onion, chopped
1 tablespoon minced hot green chilies
2 tablespoons peanut oil
½ teaspoon salt
½ cup coconut milk (page 120)
2 tablespoons peanut butter

Wash spinach and steam in saucepan (with only the water clinging to the leaves after washing) until tender. Sauté onions and chilies in peanut oil for a few minutes. Mix peanut butter with coconut milk and add to onion mixture. Add cooked spinach and salt. Cook and stir for 5 minutes. Serve hot.

GROUNDNUT SAUCE

    1 cup roasted peanuts, shelled, skinned and mashed
    2 cups water
    2 tablespoons cooking oil
    ½ teaspoon salt
    ⅛ teaspoon ground red chili pepper
    2 tablespoons onion, minced

Put peanuts, water, salt and chili pepper in saucepan. Simmer for 10 minutes. Sauté onion in oil until yellow and add to sauce. Stir well and simmer for another 10 minutes. Serve hot in gravy boat as accompaniment to boiled potatoes.

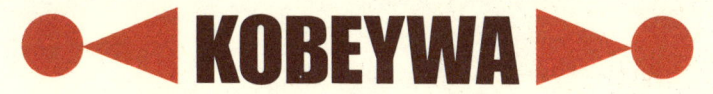

KOBEYWA
(okra sauce)

    1 pound okra, washed, chopped fine
    2 cups water
    1 teaspoon baking soda
    1 teaspoon salt
    1 tomato, chopped
    ¼ teaspoon ground red chili pepper

Prepare okra and put into a strainer. Add soda to water and bring to a boil. Steam okra over boiling water until tender. Put into a saucepan. Add salt, tomato and red pepper and simmer for 10 minutes. Serve hot with any of the "mashes".

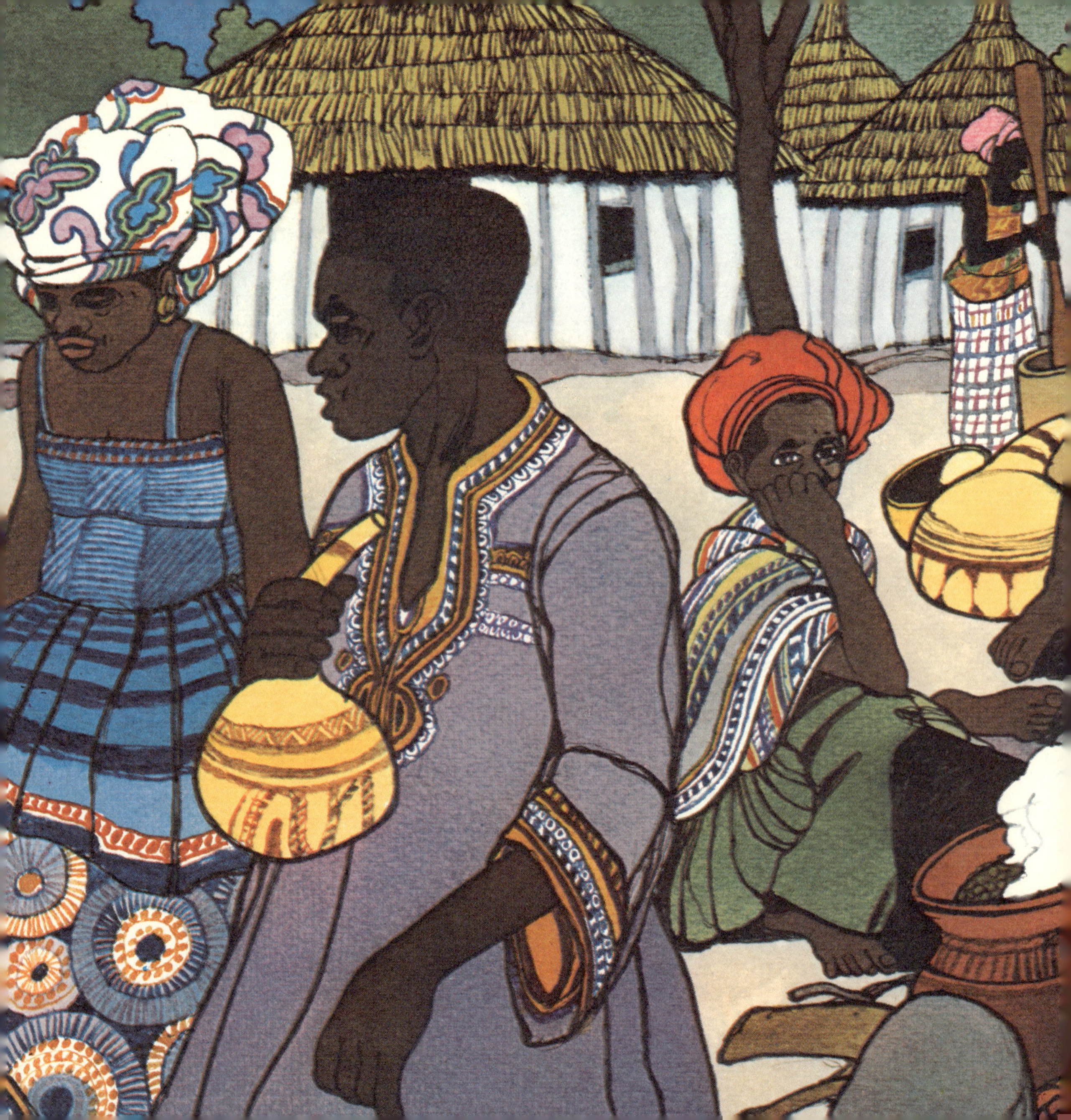

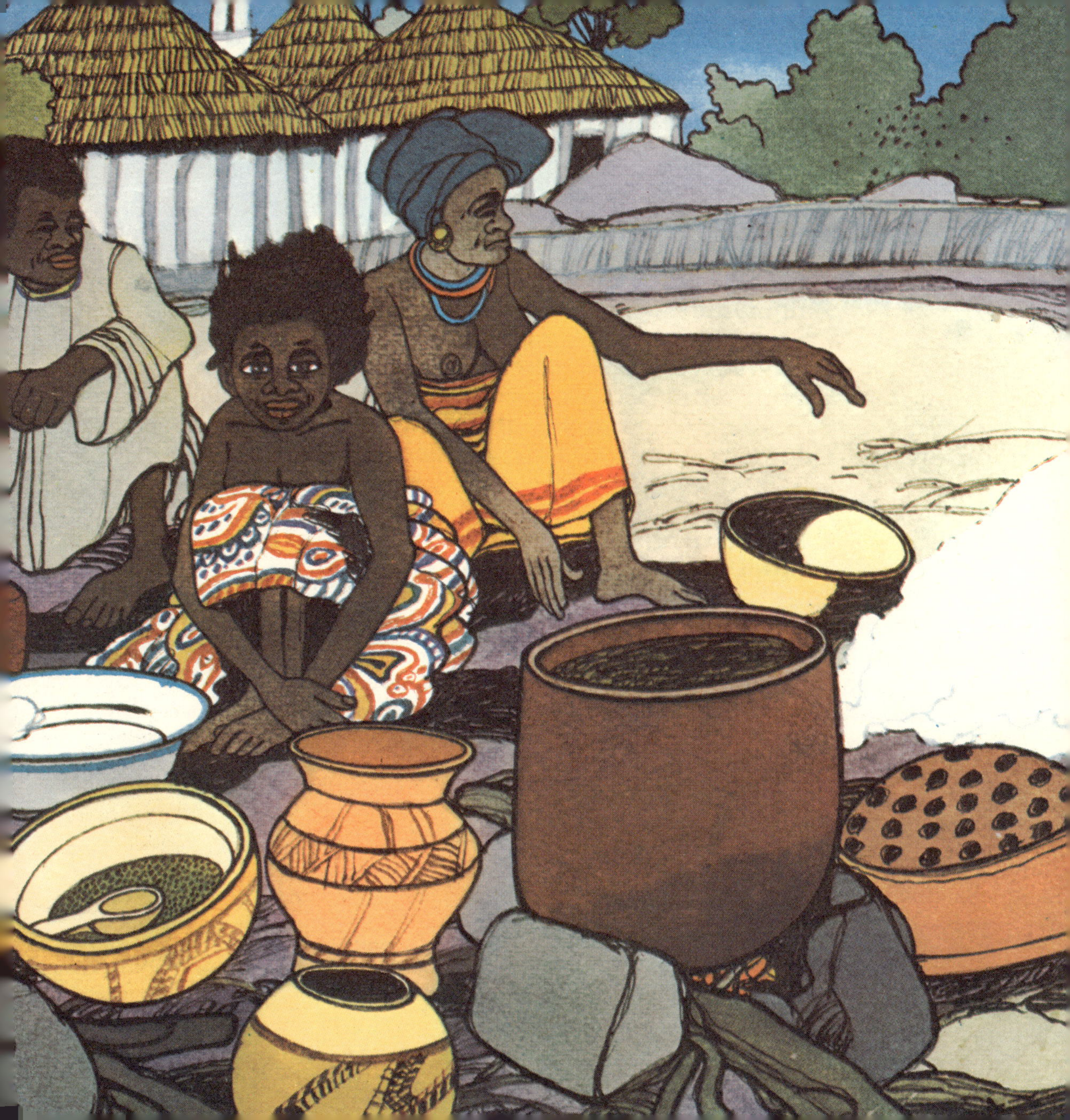

PALAVA

(spinach sauce)

- 1 pound fresh spinach
- 1 cup water
- ½ cup cooked meat, minced
- ½ cup fish (smoked, dried or canned), minced
- 2 fresh tomatoes, chopped
- 2 medium-size onions, chopped
- 1 hot green chili pepper, seeded and minced
- 4 tablespoons butter or margarine
- ¼ teaspoon paprika
- 1 teaspoon salt
- 2 small hard-cooked eggs, chopped fine

Wash and chop spinach. Cook in 1 cup water until tender. Pour off stock and save. Sauté chopped onions, tomatoes, eggs and chili pepper for 10 minutes. Add bits of meat and fish. Season with salt and pepper. Add spinach, stock and paprika, stirring well. Simmer for 15 minutes. Serve hot with "mashes" or boiled potatoes.

PALAVA

Sierra Leone

- ¼ pound tripe
- 2 cups water
- 1 teaspoon salt
- 1 pound boneless beef stew meat, cut into bite-size pieces
- 1½ cups peanut oil (palm oil is better if you can get it)
- 1½ pounds fresh spinach, chard or collard greens (or a mixture)
- ½ pound smoked fish
- 1 cup cooked, mashed red beans (canned Mexican refried beans are good)
- 4 green onions, chopped
- 1 teaspoon cayenne pepper

Wash tripe thoroughly in cold water. Drain. Cover with salted water and simmer for 5 hours. Drain, cool and slice into thin slices. Put 2 cups of water into a deep stewpot together with the salt, beef, oil and prepared tripe. Simmer covered for 45 minutes. While this is simmering wash the spinach, and steam in another pan with a small amount of water, until tender. Drain, chop and set aside. Add beans and fish, onions and cayenne to the stew pot. Put spinach on top and simmer uncovered for another half-hour or more until the water is nearly all steamed off and only the oil and the other ingredients remain. Serve hot with one of the "mashes."

CURRIED MEAT SAUCE

   3 tablespoons peanut oil
   1 pound lean ground beef
   1 large onion, chopped
   1 clove garlic, minced
   2 cups water
   1 large potato, peeled, diced
   2 fresh tomatoes, peeled, chopped
   3 tablespoons curry powder
   1 teaspoon salt
½ cup water
   2 tablespoons flour

Brown meat in oil. Add onion and garlic and brown. Add water, potato, tomatoes, curry powder and salt. Cook until potato is tender. Make a paste of the flour and water and add it to the boiling sauce, stirring and cooking until thickened. Serve on rice.

PILLI PILLI

(red pepper sauce)

  2 cups tomato sauce
  ¼ cup onion, peeled, minced fine
  1 small clove garlic, peeled, minced fine
  Juice of 1 lemon
  1 teaspoon ground red chili pepper
  1 tablespoon grated horseradish

Mix all ingredients together and blend. Store in covered jar in refrigerator. Serve with cold, cooked shelled shrimp or prawns.

PILLI PILLI MAYONNAISE

Add 1 tablespoon of the above sauce to 1 cup of mayonnaise (page 29).

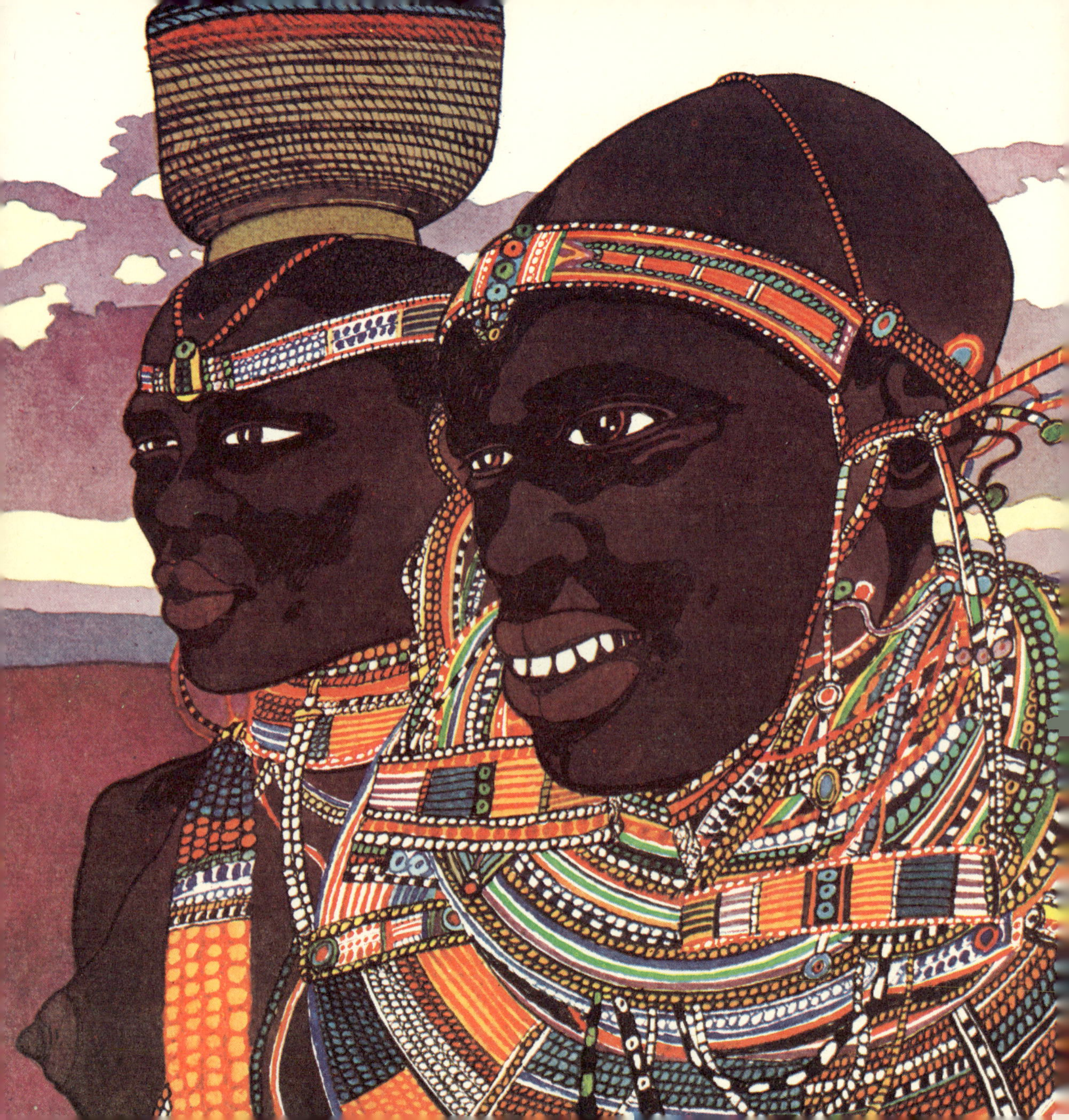

◄ RED CHUTNEY ►

- 4 fresh tomatoes, peeled and chopped
- 1 tablespoon minced candied ginger
- ½ large onion, chopped fine
- ½ cup vinegar
- ¼ cup white sugar
- ¼ cup brown sugar
- 1 teaspoon salt
- 1 teaspoon chili powder
- ½ lemon, sliced thin
- ½ orange, sliced thin
- ½ cup raisins

Combine all ingredients in saucepan. Mix well. Simmer 20 minutes or until quite thick. Serve cold.

◄ GREEN CHUTNEY ►

- 2 cups coconut, fresh-grated or packaged
- 4 green chili peppers, seeded and minced
- 1 cup minced parsley (Chinese is best if available)
- 1 teaspoon sugar
- 1 teaspoon salt
- Juice of 1 lime
- 1 cup plain yogurt

Combine all ingredients. Mix thoroughly. Let stand for several hours before serving. Good with roasted meat.

PAPAYA CHUTNEY

- 2 cups peeled, coarsely chopped papaya
- 1 cup water
- 1 cup pitted, chopped dates
- 1 tablespoon peanut oil
- 1 hot green chili, seeded, minced
- ¼ teaspoon salt
- 2 tablespoons sugar
- ½ cup raisins
- 1 teaspoon ground cumin
- 3 tablespoons lemon juice
- 1 tablespoon brandy (optional)

Combine papaya and water and soak for 15 minutes. Sauté chili in oil for 2 or 3 minutes. Drain papaya and reserve liquid. Add drained papaya and dates to chili and cook for 2 to 3 minutes. Add raisins, salt, sugar and papaya water. Simmer uncovered until papaya is tender. Stir in cumin, lemon juice and brandy. Remove from heat. Cool. Store in refrigerator in glass jar.

TAMBOULE

½ cup dry couscous or ground wheat, crushed
3 scallions, chopped fine
1 cup minced Chinese parsley
1 cup minced parsley
½ cup minced fresh mint leaves
   or 2 tablespoons dried mint leaves ground in a mortar

Soak couscous in water for ½ hour. Drain well and mix with green things.

ADD:

½ cup olive oil
½ teaspoon salt
½ teaspoon pepper
4 tablespoons lemon juice

Mix again. Serve with cold sliced meats or cold seafood.

◀ HOT CARROT RELISH ▶

 1 pound carrots, washed, peeled and minced
 1 tablespoon minced fresh ginger
 1 clove garlic, minced
 1½ cups sugar, boiled with ½ cup water
 1 teaspoon salt
 ¾ cup vinegar
 1 teaspoon ground red chili pepper
 Seeds from 2 cardamom pods, crushed

Prepare carrots. Crush ginger, garlic and cardamom seeds. Bring sugar to boil with ½ cup of water. Add carrots, chili pepper, ginger, cardamom seeds, garlic and salt. Cook for 15 minutes. Add vinegar and cook, stirring constantly, until thick. Chill.

◀ CUCUMBER SAMBAL ▶

Peel 3 fresh cucumbers. Grate them into a bowl. Sprinkle a teaspoonful of salt over them and let stand for an hour. Drain. Add 1 tablespoon vinegar and ⅛ teaspoon chili powder. Good with curried dishes.

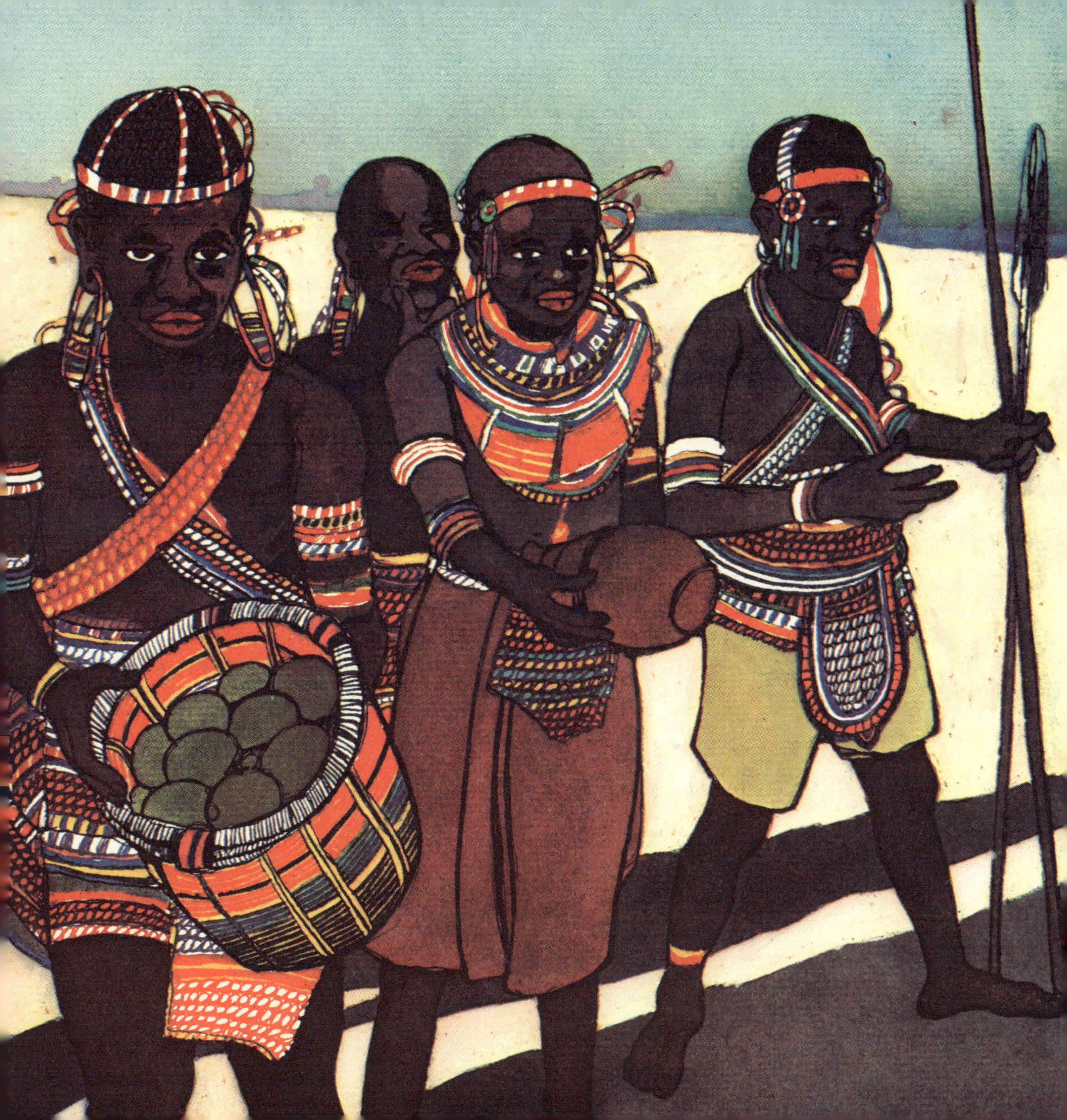

TAPIOCA

  2½ cups coconut milk (page 120)
    2 eggs, separated
    6 tablespoons sugar
  ⅛ teaspoon salt
    4 tablespoons quick-cooking tapioca
    1 teaspoon nutmeg, freshly grated

Prepare coconut milk. If made with packaged instead of fresh coconut, you will have to prepare it the night before you make the pudding. Beat egg whites until foamy. Add sugar and nutmeg and beat until stiff. Set aside. Mix egg yolks, coconut milk, tapioca and salt. Bring to a boil over medium heat stirring constantly. Remove from heat immediately. Pour hot mixture slowly into beaten egg mixture, stirring hard and folding it in as you pour. Cool for 15 minutes. Stir again. Put into individual serving bowls. Chill. Sprinkle with a little more grated nutmeg before serving.

TOP BANANAS

Peel and cut hard sweet bananas (one per person) in half lengthwise. Fry in small amount of butter until golden brown on both sides. Sprinkle generously with sugar and lemon juice while frying and just before serving sprinkle a little freshly grated nutmeg on top.

BANANA BOATS

- 4 large bananas
- 1 cup chopped fresh (or canned crushed) pineapple
- ½ cup heavy cream, whipped
- 1 tablespoon sugar
- ½ cup chopped peanuts

With damp clean cloth wipe skins of bananas. With sharp knife cut a 1-inch lengthwise strip out of inside curve of each banana. Discard strip. Scoop out pulp with spoon. Chop pulp and add drained pineapple. Whip the cream adding 1 tablespoon of sugar as you whip. Put banana skins on shallow plate. Fill with fruit mixture. Top with whipped cream. Sprinkle with peanuts. Serve cold.

MANGO MOUSSE

2 cups fresh mango slices
   or 1 (16-oz.) can mango slices, drained
1 cup heavy cream, whipped
4 tablespoons powdered sugar
½ cube semi-sweet chocolate, grated fine

Wash mangoes and cut into pieces without peeling. Simmer gently until tender in enough water to cover. (Canned mangoes need no cooking.) Put through sieve or food mill. Cool pulp. Fold in whipped cream and powdered sugar. Put into a serving dish. Garnish with chocolate. Chill.

COCONUT PUDDING

East Africa

2 eggs
1½ tablespoons sugar
1 cup coconut milk (page 120)
1 banana, peeled, mashed
½ cup fresh-grated coconut
¼ teaspoon cinnamon

Beat eggs until light. Add sugar and beat. Add coconut milk slowly, beating as you add. Add banana and beat. Add coconut. Stir well. Pour into buttered baking dish. Sprinkle with cinnamon. Bake at 350° for 45 minutes. Serve hot or chilled.

BANANA CREPES

    4 ripe bananas, peeled, chopped
    2 eggs, separated
    4 tablespoons flour
    1 teaspoon lemon juice
    2 teaspoons sugar
      Butter or oil for frying
      Powdered sugar for topping
      Lemon juice for topping

Mash bananas and stir until smooth. Beat egg yolks and add flour and lemon juice. Add to bananas and stir well. Beat egg whites until stiff. Fold in sugar. Add to banana mixture. Heat about a teaspoonful of butter or oil in a frying pan until hot. Drop crêpe mixture by the tablespoonful into the hot pan and fry until brown on both sides, turning carefully with a spatula (the crêpes are very delicate and should be no more than 3 inches in diameter for easy turning). Drain on paper towels. Sprinkle with powdered sugar and drops of lemon juice. Serve immediately. Makes about 2 dozen.

MACAROONS

⅓ cup condensed milk
1¼ cups moist, grated coconut
1 egg white
Pinch of salt
½ cup minced peanuts
½ teaspoon vanilla

Soak coconut in condensed milk for a few minutes. Beat egg white until stiff. Fold egg white into coconut mixture. Add salt, peanuts and vanilla. Stir until well mixed. Drop tablespoons of the batter onto greased cookie sheet. Bake at 250° for 20 to 30 minutes until golden. Makes 12 medium-size macaroons.

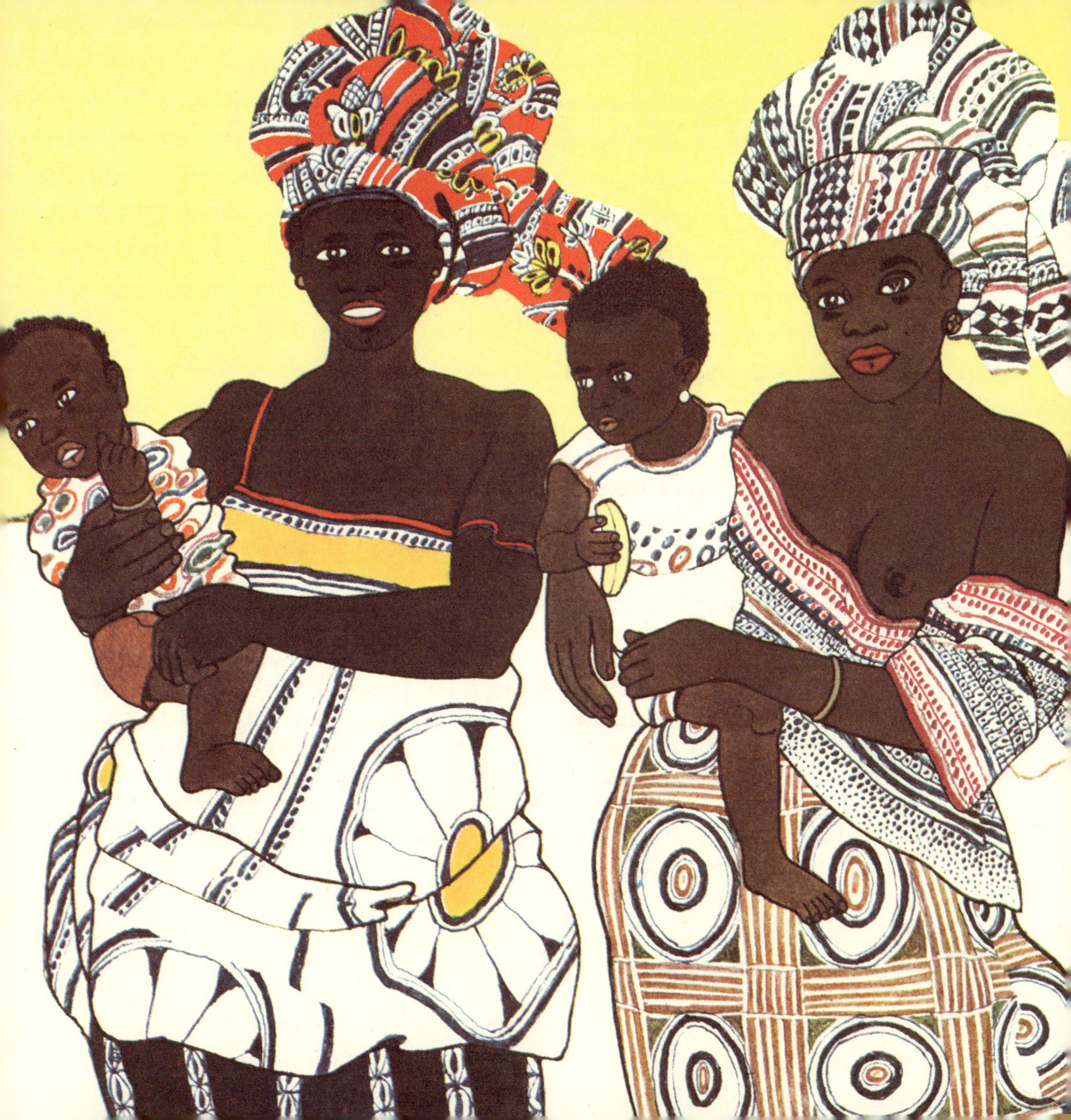

PUFF PUFFS

(raised dough balls)

2 cups flour
1 yeast cake (5/8 oz.)
½ cup milk
2 eggs, beaten
½ cup sugar
1 teaspoon nutmeg
1 teaspoon vanilla
3 cups peanut oil for deep-fat frying

Sift flour into large mixing bowl. Dissolve crumbled yeast cake in ½ cup lukewarm milk. Do not let milk get hot. Combine beaten eggs, sugar, nutmeg, vanilla and yeast mixture. Make a well in flour and slowly stir in wet mixture to form soft dough. Cover bowl with a thin clean cloth and set in a warm place to rise. Let dough rise until double in bulk (an hour or more). Heat oil in heavy pot to deep-fat frying temperature (375°). Using teaspoon, shape dough into small balls and drop into boiling oil a few at a time. Dip teaspoon in cold water after each shaping to keep dough from sticking. Fry balls to golden brown. Remove with slotted spoon. Drain on paper towels. Sprinkle with sugar and serve hot. Makes 2 dozen.

◀ GALI AKPONO ▶

(corn meal cookies)

- 1 cup white corn meal
- 1½ cups flour
- ¾ cup sugar
- ¼ teaspoon salt
- 1 cube (4-oz.) margarine
- 2 eggs (reserve one white for brushing cookie tops)
- ¼ cup milk
- ½ teaspoon freshly grated nutmeg or grated rind of two limes

Dampen corn meal with 2 tablespoons water. Sift flour, sugar and salt together and add. Rub margarine into dry mixture. Beat eggs lightly, reserving 1 white, and add. Add milk and mix. Add nutmeg or lime rind. Roll dough out to ¼-inch thickness. Cut into 3-inch rounds. Mark edges with fork. Place on cookie sheet. Brush tops with beaten egg white. Bake at 350° for 15 minutes or until golden brown. Makes 2 dozen.

CHIN CHIN

(deep fried cakes)

¾ cup flour
1 teaspoon baking powder
1 tablespoon sugar
½ teaspoon cinnamon
Pinch of salt
1 tablespoon grated lemon peel
1 tablespoon grated orange peel
1 egg, beaten
1 tablespoon melted butter or margarine
Peanut oil for deep frying

Sift dry ingredients together into bowl. Add orange and lemon peel, egg and shortening. Mix to form soft dough. Knead for a few minutes on floured pastry board, adding more flour if necessary to make dough firm and smooth. Cover with cloth and let rise in warm place for 30 minutes. Roll out on floured board to ½-inch thickness. Cut into 1½-inch triangles. Heat oil to deep frying temperature. Drop cakes into oil a few at a time frying until they are brown. Drain on paper towels. Sprinkle with powdered sugar. Serve hot. Makes 2 dozen.

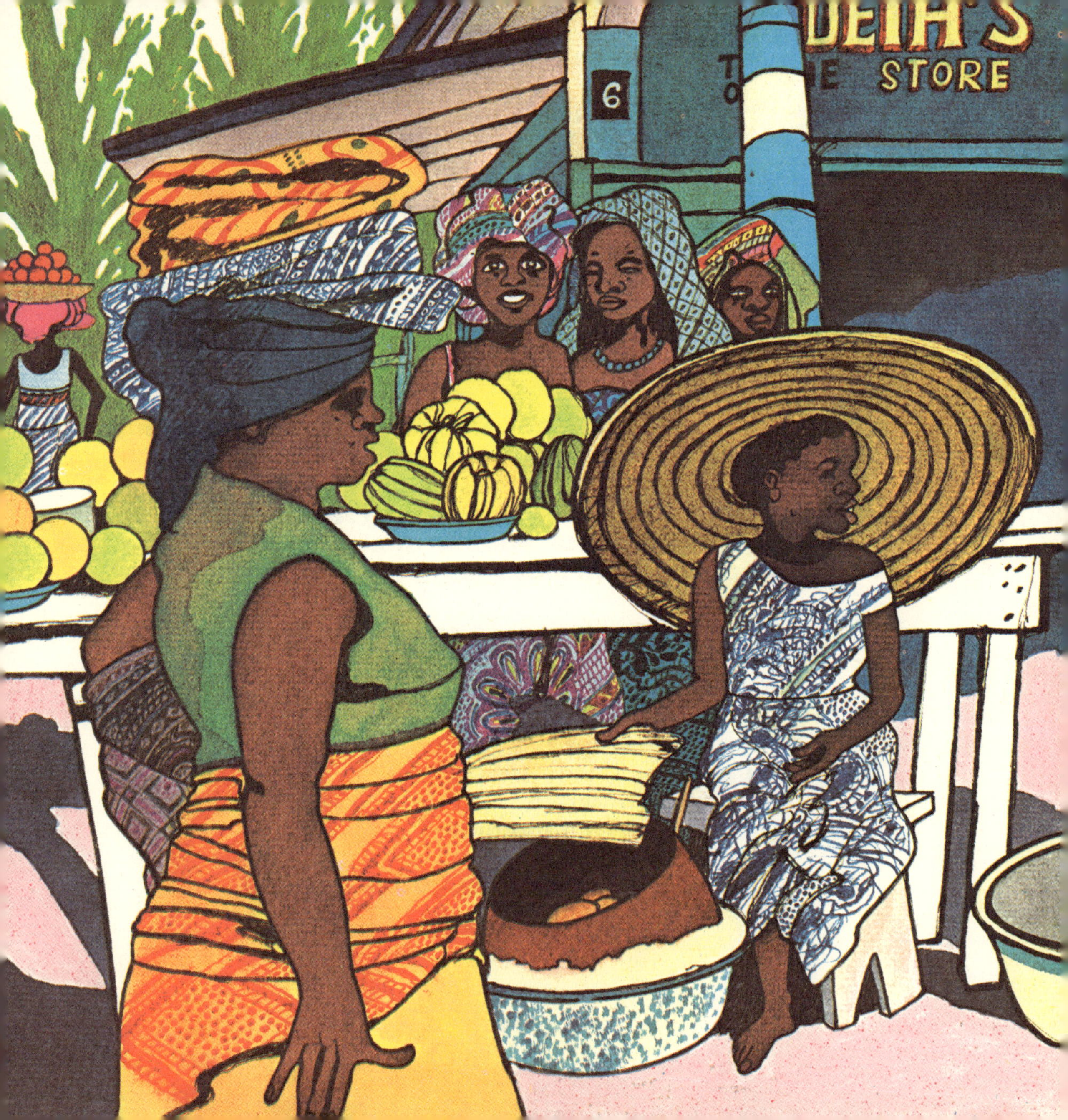
DEITH'S
STORE
6

◀ APRICOT CREAM ▶

  2 cups packaged dried apricots
2½ cups water
  ½ cup sugar (or according to sweetness of fruit)
  ½ cup heavy cream, whipped
  ½ teaspoon vanilla
  2 tablespoons sugar

Soak apricots overnight in water. Do not drain. Add ½ cup sugar and cook over low heat, stirring frequently until water is almost absorbed, being careful not to scorch. Put mixture through a food mill or a blender. Chill. Whip cream, adding 2 tablespoons sugar and vanilla. Fold into apricot mixture. Chill. Top with spoonful of whipped cream if desired.

◀ FRUIT WHIP ▶

4 eggs, separated
½ cup sugar
4 bananas, mashed
2 cups crushed pineapple
1 cup orange juice
   Whipped cream and shredded coconut

Beat egg yolks and ¼ cup sugar until frothy. Add fruit and juice and mix. Pour into freezer pans and let freeze until mushy. Beat egg whites and ¼ cup sugar until stiff. Fold into fruit mixture. Return to pans and freeze until firm. Top with whipped cream and shredded coconut.

◀ GROUNDNUT PASTRY ▶

- 2 cups sifted flour
- 1 teaspoon salt
- 2 tablespoons sugar
- 4 tablespoons pulverized peanuts
- 10 tablespoons shortening (preferably half butter)
- 1 egg
- 3 tablespoons ice water
- Few drops lemon juice

Sift flour, salt and sugar into mixing bowl. Stir in peanuts. Add shortening and blend with fingertips until flaky. Beat egg slightly with a fork and mix with ice water. Combine lemon juice and water mixture and add to the flour mixture slowly, mixing and tossing the flour with a fork, until dough is formed. Divide dough into 2 equal parts. Chill for 10 minutes. Roll out between two pieces of waxed paper. Makes two 9-inch crusts.

► PUMPKIN PIE ◄

Ghana

- 3 cups cooked pumpkin
- 2 eggs, beaten
- 1 (13-oz.) can evaporated milk
- ½ cup white sugar
- ½ cup brown sugar
- 1 tablespoon flour
- ½ teaspoon salt
- ½ teaspoon ginger
- ¼ teaspoon cloves
- ¼ teaspoon nutmeg
- 1 teaspoon cinnamon
- 1 unbaked groundnut pie crust (page 115)
- ¼ cup pulverized peanuts

Spoon pumpkin into deep bowl. Add eggs and milk and mix. Add sugar and mix. Sift flour, salt and spices together. Add to pumpkin mixture and beat. Pour into a pastry-lined pie tin. Sprinkle with peanuts. Bake at 350° for 50 minutes or more until pie filling puffs up and cracks open a bit.

SWEET POTATO PIE

     3 large sweet potatoes
     3 tablespoons butter
    ½ cup hot milk
     2 eggs, separated
    ½ cup sugar
    ½ teaspoon salt
    ¼ teaspoon nutmeg
     1 tablespoon brandy (or ½ teaspoon vanilla)
     1 unbaked groundnut pie crust (page 115)

Boil sweet potatoes until tender, peel and mash. Melt butter in the hot milk and add to potatoes. Beat until soft and creamy. Beat egg whites until stiff and set aside. Add beaten egg yolks, sugar, salt, nutmeg and brandy to potato mixture and mix well. Fold in egg whites. Pour filling into crust. Bake at 350° for 30 minutes.

COCONUT CAKE

¾ cup flour
2 teaspoons baking powder
6 tablespoons margarine
½ cup sugar

¼ cup milk
2 eggs, beaten
½ cup grated fresh coconut

ICING

2 egg whites
½ cup sugar
4 tablespoons honey
Pinch of salt
½ teaspoon vanilla
¼ cup grated fresh coconut for topping

Sift flour and baking powder together and rub the margarine into the sifted ingredients with the back of a serving spoon until the mixture has the consistency of crumbs. Add sugar and mix. Combine eggs and milk and add gradually to creamed mixture. Beat until quite smooth. Add coconut and mix well. Put into a greased 9-inch round cake tin. Bake at 350° for 30 to 40 minutes. Cool on a rack.

Put unbeaten egg whites, sugar, honey and salt into top of a double boiler over hot water. Beat with rotary beater while bringing the water to a boil. Keep beating 7 minutes after water boils. Remove from heat. Add vanilla. Beat until icing stands in firm peaks. Frost cake. Sprinkle coconut on top.

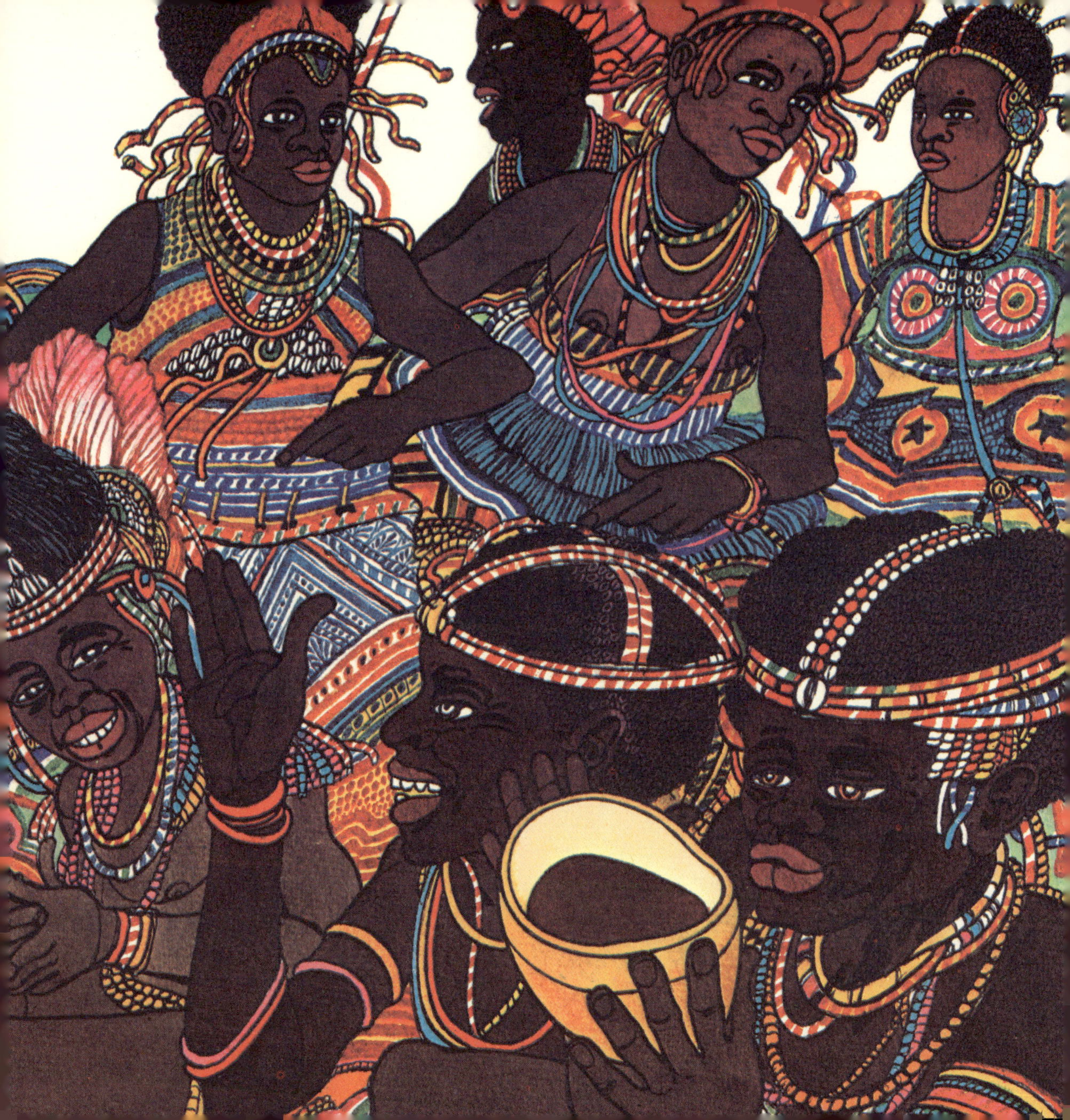

◀ COCONUT MILK ▶

(for use in vegetable dishes, stews and desserts)

WITH FRESH COCONUT

Remove shells and peel meat of two coconuts. Grate meat. Put into bowl. Add 3½ cups very hot water. Mix well and let stand for ½ hour. Put into a strainer over a mixing bowl. Squeeze coconut with your hand and press juice out against strainer. Discard coconut meat. Makes 3 cups.

WITH PACKAGED COCONUT

Put 1 (3½-oz.) package (1½ cups) coconut into a bowl. Pour 3 cups milk over it. Refrigerate overnight. Drain off milk. Put coconut in strainer and squeeze and press remaining milk out. Discard coconut. Makes 2½ cups coconut milk.

WHITE ELEPHANT

Congo

2 cups coconut milk (page 120)
2 tablespoons sugar
6 ounces white rum
6 ounces white Creme de Cacao
1 cup crushed ice

Blend all ingredients in blender or shaker until smooth. Sprinkle with fresh-grated nutmeg and serve over a tablespoonful of crushed ice.

PARTY PUNCH

Ethiopia (nonalcoholic)

1 cup orange juice
1 cup lemon juice
1 cup pineapple juice
2 cups white grape juice
1 cup raspberry syrup
2½ quarts club soda

Mix all ingredients in order given in large punch bowl. Makes 1 gallon.

◄ PINEAPPLE COOLER ►

Ghana

Peelings from 1 fresh pineapple
1 quart boiling water
1 cup chopped pineapple
3 cloves
Peelings from half an orange
Sugar to taste

Twist off top of pineapple and discard. Wash pineapple and cut in half, then in quarters, then eighths. Peel sections setting fruit aside. Prepare 1 cup chopped fruit. Put peelings, chopped fruit, cloves and orange peelings into a bowl or jar. Add boiling water. Cover and let stand for 24 hours. Strain. Sweeten to taste. Pour over ice cubes and serve with a sprig of fresh mint on top. (Gin or vodka may be added.)

◄ PINEAPPLE PUNCH ►

   1 cup sugar
1½ cups water
   2 sticks cinnamon
10 whole cloves
   3 cups pineapple juice
   1 cup orange juice
   1 cup lemon juice
   Crushed ice

Put sugar, water, cinnamon and cloves into a saucepan and bring to a boil. Boil 5 minutes. Remove cinnamon and cloves. Put pineapple, orange and lemon juice into large bowl. Add sugar syrup. Stir well and serve over crushed ice. Serves 8.

PUNCH OUAGA

In a punch bowl put mango slices from 2 mangoes, 2 slices of fresh pineapple, slices from 2 peeled bananas. Add 1 pint of white rum, ¼ teaspoon vanilla, 1½ cups sugar syrup*, 1 pint pineapple juice, 1 pint grapefruit juice. Mix well. Just before serving add 1 quart quinine water. Serve ice-cold. Makes about 3 quarts.

*Sugar syrup: Add 3 cups sugar to 1 cup boiling water, stir and boil for 5 minutes. Cool.

OROMBO

Juice of 6 oranges or 3 grapefruit
4 cups hot water   4 tablespoons sugar

Put juice in pitcher. Add water and sugar. Cool. Serve with ice cubes. (Gin, rum or vodka may be added.)

LEMON SQUASH

Juice of 3 lemons or 3 limes
3 tablespoons sugar   2 cups water

Put juice in pitcher. Add sugar and stir. Add water. Serve with ice cubes. (Gin, rum or vodka may be added.)

FROSTED COCOA

1 tablespoon cocoa
1 cup milk
1 egg
Sugar to taste

Mix cocoa with enough milk to make a smooth paste. Bring remaining milk to a boil. Remove from fire, stir in paste and cool. Separate the egg. Beat the yolk and add to cocoa mixture. Add sugar to taste. Pour into glass and chill. Beat egg white until frothy, adding a little sugar as you beat, and top the drink with it. Makes 1 serving.

HOT COCOA

1 teaspoon cocoa
1 cup milk
Sugar to taste

Make a paste of cocoa and a little cold milk in a saucepan. Heat remaining milk and pour slowly over cocoa paste while stirring. Add sugar and serve at once. Makes 1 serving.